Canadian Paratrooper
to Skydiver

SEAN J GILLIGAN

Canadian Paratrooper
Copyright © 2020 by Sean J Gilligan

All rights reserved. No part of this publication may be reproduced, distributed, or transmitted in any form or by any means, including photocopying, recording, or other electronic or mechanical methods, without the prior written permission of the author, except in the case of brief quotations embodied in critical reviews and certain other non-commercial uses permitted by copyright law.

Tellwell Talent
www.tellwell.ca

ISBN
978-0-2288-2555-5 (Paperback)
978-0-2288-2556-2 (eBook)

Prologue: This is the story of my years spent as a Canadian paratrooper, the challenges and tribulations of a soldier during the Cold War era. I was born into a life of constant challenges, my early years in the province of Ontario, spent mainly on a rural farm near Ottawa, Ontario. After several years spent in several infantry battalions, I was sent to #3 Commando, The Canadian Airborne Regiment. This is basically the story of what I endured for the three years I spent as a paratrooper and the lasting effect it had on my life. After my release from the Canadian Armed Forces, I kept my interest in certain military skills, like parachuting and hunting.

In the Cold war era parachuting continued on a smaller basis, as parachute companies integrated into the regular infantry battalions. Then in 1968, The Canadian Airborne Regiment was created, absorbing these smaller, dispersed units into one entity, based in Edmonton, Alberta. In 1978 this regiment was relocated to Petawawa, Ontario, while the Airborne training center remained in Edmonton, the main airport "airhead" stationed in Trenton, Ontario. The ultimate goal was to create an elite Special Force, termed the SSF (Special Service Force), a brigade (5000 men), capable of fighting anywhere in the country, or the world at short notice.

Fifteen years after it was created, I joined the new Commando of the Airborne. After I jumped from a C-130 Hercules in late November of 1983, I would never be the same guy again. I survived that early ordeal and others, continuing to this day as a member of CSPA, the civilian parachuting entity. Ultimately, The Canadian Airborne Regiment was disbanded in 1994, after the fiasco in Somalia, serving as a United Nations peacekeeping force. All the expertise accumulated for decades was lost to the winds. Later NDHQ in Ottawa, realized the urgent need for Airborne trained soldiers, as every modern nation in the world utilizes them. Today decades later, each of Canada's three infantry battalions has one jump company. Also, JTF-2 is Canada's equivalent of NATO Special Forces, all members are parachute qualified and trained in a variety of special force skills. They were used in Iraq and Syria primarily as advisors to the Kurdish fighters to defeat ISIS, later moving into Syria, while all other Canadian units returned home after ISIS were defeated and their caliphate vanished in Iraq.

The author spent three of twelve years service in The Canadian Army as an airborne soldier. Most Airborne soldiers consider themselves a brotherhood, an elite, highly trained cadre of men, able to handle the stress and demands to accomplish any task. Failure or second place is not an option, the training meant to eliminate those who can not meet the exacting standards required. It is the same for the U.S. Navy's Seals, the Army Rangers, 82nd Airborne Division, the U.K. Special Forces (SAS, SBS), the French Foreign Legion or the German Falchirmjagger. The days of conventional warfare are over it seems. To combat terrorists in unconventional warfare, insurrections in the Middle East, small units of highly trained soldiers is the way to go. This concept has been used before, displaying that a few "good men" can achieve goals that are impossible for larger, conventional division sized units. It will be seen that The Canadian Airborne Regiment specialized in small unit, behind the lines operations during the 1970's-80's, frequently succeeding against much larger forces.

The final chapter will deal with near death experiences. These traumatic events may hit at anytime, whether one is a soldier or civilian, no matter what the circumstances. The author experienced these stressful events, before, during and after military service. The goal is to learn from each event, to improve existing skills and not to be intimidated. To maintain one's lifestyle and relevance in life, success is pushing on, for as The Airborne say, "It's time to put up or shut up. I will never quit, I will fight on to my last breath, even if I am bleeding to death, lying on my back. My brothers demand it, those heroes who came before me are watching from afar."

The Selection

In late June 1983, I went through Initial Selection with about 30 other recruit paras. By August, I had lost about 25 pounds and survived, along with one other soldier, Trooper Hall. What is Selection you may ask. It is a word used in Airborne Special Forces throughout the Western world. It had been thrust into my lap suddenly that month, due to an urgent need for Airborne recruits. My dad dropped me off at CFB Petawawa that day, driving from my home in Ottawa, Ontario, 100 miles to the south. I reported to RCR Battle School first, where young soldiers begin infantry training. The senior course officer after reviewing my personal file considered promoting me to instructor. At this point I was a trained infantryman with eight-years service. Originally, I entered the service as an infantryman, my chosen specialty after being refused my primary choice of jet fighter pilot. My uncle Connor was one of my mentors then. He was a pilot in the RCAF, flying mainly Hercules transports, advising me to try for pilot.

The highlight for me so far, was my first overseas deployment to then West Germany in 1979. I was posted to N Company, 3rd Battalion RCR, based in CFB Baden-Soellingen, Bavaria. Two other soldiers, my buddies Ian Wadleigh and Joel Sorbie were also with me. Later all three of us became Airborne paratroopers. I started that deployment as a 19-year-old kid and emerged as a trained soldier. It was a blast, I loved Germany, good beer, frauleins and serious training. My unit was an integral part of 3rd CMBG, a fully mechanized bigrade, with attached armour, Leopard 1 MBT's from the RCD (Royal Canadian Dragoons). Altogether about 5000 Canadian soldiers, a small part of NATO in Europe. On one big exercise, there were around 300,000 NATO Allied soldiers and airmen. My taxi into battle was the M-113 Armoured personnel carrier, containing a section of ten men theoretically at least.

I had my first injury after about a month. It was during a live fire assault at Sennelagger. It was reputed that this facility was built during WW2 by the German Army (Wehrmacht) and used by the Waffen SS for urban warfare training. When we went in, assaulting this mock-up village, everything was live. I carried a 7.62 mm FN C1 rifle, grenades and an M-72 anti-tank rocket launcher. I remember the adrenaline flowing as we ran and crawled toward the village, firing in two man teams. Fire and movement, sprinting in short spurts, then hitting the ground and firing at our targets, heaving grenades and firing the M-72 which had a range of about 200 yards/meters. Overhead artillery shells whined, and 81 mm mortar shells exploded to our front. Machine guns chattered off to our flank, striking the village buildings, sending red tracers arcing into the sky. I felt the concussion waves from the explosions, smelt the cordite as my platoon closed on the objective. Finally, it was over, then my platoon gathered to be debriefed by our leaders, the CSM and platoon officer. One of my mates remarked then, "Hey Gill, what happened to your leg?" I looked down and saw my combat pants were ripped.

"Oh...don't know." We were smoking cigarettes, catching our breath and drinking from our canteens. "Probably jumping over the wire obstacle," I remarked nonchalantly. I opened the tear and stared at my leg, stunned at what I saw. My right knee cap was split open, with a piece of meat dangling from it, blood slowly oozing down my leg. It was a surprise, as I had felt no pain during the whole time. The CSM (Company Sergeant Major) looked at it, then ordered me medi-evacked to the nearest hospital. It was run by the British as I found out. Two nurses looked at it, then gave me a brush to clean it, as muck was ground into it. Then the pain started! In the end, they gave me a scalpel, which I used to cut off the dangling chunk of flesh. That hurt, as they told me it would leave a permanent scar. "No kidding? That is what I want!"

Next day I was told to report to the medic at the MIR three times a day to get my wound treated. I think a day later we were told (N Coy) that we were doing infantry-armour co-operative training. I brushed aside the MIR thing, reporting for duty. We drove Leopard 1 tanks, some operation of the turret and main 105 mm gun, learned its weak spots so we could disable it, or blow it (or any Russian enemy tanks) if the shit hit the fan. This was the Cold War. We knew the East Bloc outnumbered us in tanks at least 3-1. At lunch that day I reported to the CSM. "Gilligan where are you supposed to be?" I stared up at the hulking 6-foot plus CSM nervously, for he was God to me. "Ah...Ooops! Sorry Sir...the medics I think."

"Get your ass on the bus soldier. If you miss another appointment you will go to jail!" I nodded, "Yes Sir!" Off I went to the waiting bone menders a bit chagrined. At the MIR, a medic told me, "Know what happens if this gets infected?" I shook my head as I lay on the gurney. "We amputate your leg." Not a joke as I learned, this was serious shit.

Another incident stands out in my mind. It was later after I recuperated and returned to full duty. On an exercise, we were parked outside a German village at the start line. An American patrol jumped one of our guys at a check point. I heard he was assaulted and they stole his weapon, a SMG (9-mm sub machine gun). The company was stood to and a frantic search began throughout the town for the fugitives. Shortly after I caught them, hiding in a barn loft. I heard the squawk from their radio, giving them away. "OK come on down its over. Hands up!" I let loose a burst from my FN-C2 semi-auto rifle to accentuate the moment. Of course, they were blank rounds, but had the effect! Shortly after, I proudly marched out my first POW's before a grinning bunch of Canadian soldiers! "Well well! What do you have there Gill?"

I nodded to the Sergeant, "Two Yanks Sarge. Claim to be Long Range Recce patrol." The US soldiers were getting nervous now as a ring of angry Canadians surrounded them in the village square. After searching them, we found a looted SMG, then after terrorizing them a bit, turned them over to the Meatheads (MPs). During that Ex., I also ran into some Red Brigade terrorists or sympathisers. I was standing sentry over my section's M-113 parked inside a barn. Everyone else was in town at the local Gasthof partying. This German (NAZI bastard) came at me with a pitch fork trying to scare me. I fixed my bayonet and parried his thrust, yelling all sorts of nasty things. Then the CSM arrived to my relief, grabbed the frightened German and marched him off for a talk. So, situation diffused, I had a smoke, awaiting my relief, which came hours later, sometime early in the morning.

Back to Selection at CFB Petawawa. Standing before the CO at RCR Battle School in his office, he asked if I would like a transfer to 3 Commando, Canadian Airborne.

I was sort of surprised, pointing out that I did not have my jump wings yet.

"No problem Gilligan. That will be taken care of once you get there. They need guys now. So what do you say? If it does not work out, come back here. I will promote you as an instructor." This meant Corporal or Master Corporal at least. So, I nodded, accepted and marched out. I did not know it yet, but I was entering a new world, to say the least. It was a short walk to the Airborne lines where I duly reported to the Regimental Duty office.

After filling out paperwork, I formally cleared in to my unit, 3 Commando for processing. As I said, I was no greenhorn, but the Airborne treated me as such. As I did not have my wings, I wore the green beret and cap badge of the RCR. I drew personal weapons and para gear, then marched to the 3 Commando Barracks. Outside was a large 3 on an overhead sign. Around the Airborne Parade Square were the other two barracks for 1 and 2 Commando, the eating mess and the Airborne drinking mess. I was told most of the regiment was on leave, being early July. Off duty, I had a shower after dumping my gear in an assigned room, signed in by the Barracks NCO. "Welcome to the Borne buddy. Don't let it go to your head. Tomorrow you start earning it. If you pass Selection, pass your Basic Para, you can lose that Leg beret and wear the maroon beret. Then on to the Airborne Indoctrination course, where if you survive, you will receive the Airborne coin, making you a real paratrooper! Until then, you are a recruit...meat...nothing!"

After a shower and hitting the Eating mess, I went out to drown my misgivings in liquor. I dressed for the night, jeans and a t-shirt. I did not have an Airborne t-shirt as yet, something on my to-do list. It was a short walk across the Airborne parade square to the Kyrenia Club, the Airborne wet mess, the place where paratroopers went to relax and vent. It was a two-story building, with a bar on both levels. As this was not a busy night, with most of the regiment on leave, the main downstairs lounge was closed. So, I went upstairs and sat at the bar, ordering a beer. As I downed my beer I looked at the few other soldiers in the bar. I conversed with a few, introducing myself, saying I was just posted in. They greeted me casually, giving me a few pointers on what I was about to experience. Selection would start with a bang tomorrow, with morning PT (physical training), probably a run in PT gear. For the last month, I had been doing more running in preparation for this. I knew I had work to do, weighing in at about 195 pounds. For some reason, I had gained weight over the winter and at my age 24, this was overweight.

I awoke the next morning early, dressed in my running gear and proceeded outside for morning roll call. An NCO took our names, some 30 odd recruits, then after a bit of stretching, marched off the parade square. "Breaking into double time, OK troops! Airborne!" A chorus of shouted voices greeted this as we broke into a run. The NCO a Master-Corporal set a fast pace as we ran around the base, encouraging the ranks to keep closed. Half an hour later we returned, sweating profusely and gasping for air. After this initial run, we hit the Airborne "playground" a sort of obstacle course beside the parade square. We climbed ropes, stretched and climbed over obstacles. That day set the routine for the balance of July. After a shower and breakfast, we changed to standard olive drab combat fatigues and formed up for inspection. Then we ran across base to the armories, where we were issued our personal weapons, FN rifles, helmets and assorted fighting gear. Then loaded down with our gear we ran back to the barracks. It was rather boring routine so far, stripping our gear and weapons and cleaning. Later that day, we did our first of many marches in fighting gear, helmets and weapons. The NCOs in charge, took the occasion to tour the base pointing out important buildings to the sweating recruits. Then we descended a steep hill to the vast training area below the base. It was well known to me, as I had done years of training here with my home regiment RCR and others. I had also been a training instructor, previously during two summers with the Ceremonial Guard in Ottawa from 1980-81. This was the Mattawa Plain, a 10 kilometer stretch bordering the Ottawa River. Petawawa had existed for about a century, beginning as an artillery range before WW 1. It was the largest in Canada and was my favourite base in Canada.

We quickly learned the Airborne way of marching that month. It went from a fast walk to short runs, soon one learned to carefully adjust and tighten our fighting gear, so it did not impede one as you ran down dusty roads in the baking heat of the summer and flopped around.

That summer was hot and as August approached, the humidity increased. Anyone who has not experienced a marathon race (10-15 km plus) in 90-degree F plus heat, carrying over 60 pounds of gear, a steel pot over your head, rifle in your hands and heavy combat boots is in for a long day. That month wore on, day after day, the runs and marches getting progressively more challenging. I failed to notice our recruit platoon's shrinking numbers until there was only a handful left. Some were injured during the ground training, some quit, to be RTU'd back to where they came from. Around the start of August, this phase of Selection ended, as the full regiment was now on duty. I had survived, along with my mate Trooper Hall. The glee we experienced was short lived, as we were then assigned to our section and platoon.

I was assigned to 10 Platoon, Hall went to 12 Platoon I believe. My section commander, M/Cpl Miles greeted me that morning as we formed up for the standard parade outside the barracks for morning PT. This was a strict standard in the Borne as we called it. There were no casual days off, the Commandos either ran or marched. It was the CO, Major Leavy who ran 3 Commando and called the shots. I also met my direct superior who was

2 I/C of the section, Corporal McDonald. "Hey is that you Gilligan? What the hell are you doing here?"

"What do you think? I am posted here, just passed Initial Selection." I had met the grinning NCO that spring, inside one of my favourite watering holes in Ottawa, Molly McGuire's Irish Pub. It was also the favourite of numerous Airborne troopers on leave. I knew by now, since the Airborne Regiment had moved from their home base in Edmonton to Petawawa in the late 1970's, how they operated. Any building or bar they entered they assumed was their territory. So, that night McDonald and I got acquainted and fought outside later. It was short and a draw more or less, separated by our buddies who enjoyed the brisk scrap. Now my former pugilistic partner oversaw me! Luckily this was post Selection, by now I was down to around 178 pounds, trimming down from plus 190.

The next phase was more of the same, but continued to increase in length and pace during the runs and marches. Major Leavy and the Commando HQ were present during the big marches. CSM Irvine, had a routine of weighing our rucksacks, which were added by mid August. If it did not meet his standard, he added rocks from a big pile beside the parade square. This happened to me early to my surprise. I was labelled a C-2 gunner by Miles, therefore I carried extra gear, including the C-2 bra, worn strapped over one's chest, carrying six 30 round magazines for my heavy weapon, which also was fitted with a folding bipod. This was the extra punch each infantry section carried, usually two men, armed with the fully automatic weapons. I also knew because of their weight, they were assigned to new guys...like me.

At this point I was buoyed by my success at getting through "Initial Selection." At first, I took things lightly, thinking as the officer had said at RCR Battle School, "If things don't work out I would be glad to have you back as an instructor." But once I am faced by a challenge, it is hard for me to ignore and quit. Quitting is not in my vocabulary. Also, there was some resistance by the younger soldiers in the platoons, who by now knew I was a greenie, I did not have my wings yet, so had to wear a green beret and this was like I was wearing a red flag!

Initially it was the usual ribbing one takes as the new guy, or FNG as the army calls it. Later at the drinking messes around base it led to fisticuffs. In this I was also well attuned to. After holding my own, gradually I earned respect and after fighting half of my platoon mates it eased off. One of my early allies was "Sly" Sylvester. He was a slightly built, unintimidating guy who usually had a sly smile on his face, hence the name. What I learned was he was one of the best fighters I ever met. A former golden gloves boxer from Nova Scotia, he also had a blackbelt in the martial arts. He sort of took me under his wing, where I gradually picked up the Oriental dark arts in fighting. Just another tool for my tool box as I joked.

In fact, many of the Borne were trained in martial arts, eventually it became part of our platoon's training.

After completing morning PT, we hit the Airborne "playground." First was a rope climb of about 25-30 feet, touch the wooden beam and repel down. Then after running through the obstacle course, we paired off for sparing. This was used during WW 2, as a history buff, I knew was part of The First Special Service Force (the Devil's Brigade) and the 1st Canadian Parachute Battalion. So, it was a serious part of our training, hand-to-hand combat. Later this was used in stalking and taking out enemy sentries at night. I was also an accomplished anti-tank man by this point, adept at stalking enemy tanks and vehicles. One of the scariest methods was to hide in your foxhole/trench, let the enemy armour run over it, then emerge in its rear and take it out with a magnetic mine or shoot it in the six with an anti-tank M-72 or Karl G rocket launcher. But in the heat of battle, Canadian soldiers and others, adapted and used whatever was at hand. If nothing else, you climbed onto the tank deck and threw a grenade down the hatch.

My next big task was Mountain School in mid-August. It turned out we were not headed for Everest, but a winter resort called Calabogie near Arnprior. It was a series of mid sized hills, not really intimidating to look at. The chief instructor was Warrant Officer Gap. Also, another NCO Sergeant Mack, a Pathfinder who took the platoon up the hill on a hill hump. We wore all our combat gear, carrying weapons and rucksacks. He walked in the lead, while the rest of us ran! By the time we made it to the top, up a 45 degree slope we were gassed. During a short "smoke break" Mack and Gap smiled, not having broken a bead of sweat.

"Are you guys tired already? This is fuck all. Wait until we do some real climbing!" After humping through these rolling hills, we hit a dirt road and ran back to the chateau where we had started from. So far it was the toughest thing I had done. I found I was not there yet, as I chugged over the finish line, drenched in sweat. We were dismissed for the night, sitting around the camp area, drinking and smoking to relax. One of the mountain school soldiers training, from E Battery I believe, then entertained us by chasing some of the resort's chickens. I think he went a bit overboard though, aiming a kick at one of the prized birds. Warrant Mack saw it and intervened. "So my lad, got some excess energy to burn I see? Get yer gear on. See the top of that hill over there? Double time it up there, off you go!" We chuckled as we watched, grateful it was not us! When the sweating, cursing trooper returned he then had to repeat it...twice!

Amongst the basics of mountain warfare, we learned over the next week how to tie knots, construct 1-3 rope bridges, carry loads up and down mountains, medivac wounded off a hill, the famous slick-line 'death slide' off a cliff and free climbing. This is going up a vertical face without being roped off. One hammered pitons into a crack in the rock with a hammer, fixed a carabiner with a locked gate to it, fed your coiled rope through it and dropped the tailing edge behind you. I found out this was the toughest training I had done so far, losing more weight and dropping below 170 pounds. In a little over a month, I had shed over 30 pounds.

Finally, we were bused back to home base at the end of Mountain School. The OC, Major Leavy "the Bear" informed us at parade before our weekend off. "Men, this was to get the fat off before Fall Ex coming up. Enjoy the weekend off. Good job lads. Monday, we start at 07:00 for a little walk. Airborne!" Over 100 voices shouted Airborne Hurrah! Dismissed by our NCO's, we forgot his ominous under-stated warning almost instantly as we sprinted like children released from school for the barracks. All I focussed on was cool showers to relieve my sweating, aching body, some food and scores of cold, cold beer and hot women!

That night, I joined a group of paras as we went on a mini-pub crawl around the base. Besides our drinking mess, there were a half dozen other junior ranks messes. The "Arty Mess" I knew well, just inside the front gate and closest to the village of Petawawa. It was here on a Friday night that scores of young women gathered from all over Northern Ontario, from Renfrew in the south, Arnprior, Petawawa and North Bay to the north. By the time we hit it, all of us were well on our way to being drunk. It was a perfect late summer evening, as we danced and talked up the horde of girls packed inside. It was of course stiff competition, myself eyes and ears open, as I was learning the lay of the land. Fights erupted periodically as the Artillery and the Airborne were fierce rivals. I eventually joined a table with four of these young, attractive women. "So soldier, who are you with?" "The Borne. 3 Commando." I replied casually, trying to exude the cool confidence and humbleness Airborne are noted for.

Sly joined shortly after, my buddy boosting my fragile morale further as he told the listening women about my newly acquired black belt skills. I laughed at the smiling Sly, joined in by the giggling females. I asked what they were drinking and excusing myself headed for the bar to buy a round. Shortly after, three of my former mates from the RCR Battle School tried to butt into our new friends at our table. They were big dudes, but they made a fatal error. They laughed at Sly, who they dwarfed in stature and out-numbered 3-1, while I was still at the bar. As I returned I saw one of the hulking RCR ruffians try and shoulder Sly out of his seat.

"Oh oh!" I thought, holding my tray of drinks as I approached and halted out of range. Then Sly went into action, a flurry of arms and legs. The last dude hit the floor at my feet less than a minute later, knocked out cold! "OK...here we go ladies. Who had the Vodka and orange?" As the mess staff ejected these "losers," we calmly assured the stunned girls all was OK. I think Sly even apologized. "Sorry ladies! I just don't like being pushed.

Should have taken those fellahs outside though." He said it so calm it was a bit unnerving. That is why we loved him, a cool dependable soldier who did his job without any tangible effort. Later the two of us left with the ladies, headed for a late-night party in Pembroke...finishing in the early morning across the river in Quebec at Chez Henri Roadhouse. It was a treat for me, after enduring a blistering hot, humid summer. My approach was, I am not there yet, allot of work to do. But like sports athletes the way forward was to take it one game at a time.

As August ended, the next big hurdle to get over was Fall Con, my first big field exercise with the Airborne regiment. It began in September 19 early on a Monday morning, with 3 Commando in full battle paraphernalia on a route march off base, across the Mattawa Plain to our bivouac camp in the woods. It was a long, dusty affair in the baking heat, our four platoons marching in line astern in three ranks. One incident stood out for me. As we marched across the Mattawa Plains, once a live fire tank/artillery range, I heard a noise up ahead. At this point, we were into the march, concentrating on keeping our ranks tight as we set a fast, steady speed.

"Halt! Advance and be recognized," I heard a faint challenge from the side of the road up ahead. It took us a bit off guard, for this was not yet a tactical field exercise. We were simply on a route march to Point B, our Commando field base. Up ahead, setting the pace was our OC Major Leavy, "The Bear." It turned out the challenge came from some poor young fellah from the Militia on exercise. When this marching phalanx showed not the slightest response, he jumped onto the road before the OC holding up his hand imperiously.

"Get out of my way!" was Major Levy's response, brushing him aside like an annoying insect. After a few seconds as we absorbed this, the tense atmosphere erupted in uncontrolled laughter. Abuse and insults were heaped upon the crestfallen militiaman as our platoons surged past like a tidal wave. I almost felt pity for him as he seemed to shrink into the ground as he stood petrified at that dusty, deserted road. After about 15 kilometers we reached our objective. We broke off into platoons and carried on under our Platoon sergeant "PB McClean."

"OK boots off. Foot inspection section commanders." This was routine for me, for in the infantry, your feet were vital. I was sweating like a pig as I stripped off my gear, then sat down and took off my brand new combat boots. Then I felt the burning in my feet, looking at the soles saw strips of flesh hanging from them. After Miles, my section commander saw them, he shook his head and called in the medic. It was deemed serious enough for me to be taken off line for treatment. As it turned out, despite his efforts they got infected. The next day at the medical tent, he operated, cutting holes in the soles of my feet. I was not happy at this development, as it only increased the pain. I ended up walking/limping around the field camp using sandals from my follow-up duffle bag. This was a Borne thing, dropped off by Service Commando transport trucks, containing spare and unnecessary gear for base ops. I was given antibiotics as this was a type of trench foot. It rained periodically over the next few days, as the first week the platoons practiced small unit attacks and other field tactics. After a week or so, as the first real tactical exercise began, I was back in the platoon. I was not a 100% but felt I could muck it through.

In the last week, 3 Commando began company tactical advance to contact marches. The highlight of Ex. Bear Claw was a two-day march through a swampy wood. I heard a new lieutenant was navigating, getting us lost in the swamp for hours. My feet were still sore, wrapped inside my combat boots which were now soaked. As we struggled out of the swamp, cursing we finally hit a road, then marched all night. Most of us were dead on our feet as we trudged along. I found one could sleep while marching, in a sort of sub-conscious state. Then we heard a shot fired. Turns out, one unlucky trooper asleep like me, had wondered slowly off the road and fallen into a ditch. His mistake was his loaded FN was not on safe and his trigger caught on something and discharged, albeit a blank round. It was serious, even though no one was injured, for this was tactical, technically he gave away our position to a hypothetical enemy. His name was taken and probably charged when we returned to base after End-Ex.

Later we bumped the enemy force later that morning. Our platoon cleared a section of forest at a cross-roads, the thick foliage echoing to rapid firing guns, interspersed with loud bangs from pyrotechnics (thunder flashes, artillery simulators). Finally End-Ex was called on September 27 and we marched back to the Commando bivouac. Then we packed up our hooches (shelter halves used to make makeshift tents), loading our gear into 5-ton trucks for transport back to base. After cleaning gear and weapons, we were given leave for a few days.

The final part of Selection was a Pre-Para course lasting about three weeks from October 24 to 4 November. I reported to the base gym for this, along with about 50 other recruits for the Basic Para course. The good part was I was excused normal platoon routine, no extra duties or other stuff the army threw at one to piss you off. The Pre-Para consisted of allot of PT, daily runs of progressively longer and faster duration. By now, I was in the zone though, confident, determined and aggressive. My buddy Ian Wadleigh, who I had known from the reserves and Germany, now a trucker in Service Commando saw me off before I left for Edmonton. "Either I return with my wings or you will never see me again!"

I said that jokingly, confident I was that I would pass the course. We drank beer in the mess the final night, discussing this vital point in my military career. "Dude if you fuck this up I will kill you myself!" Wads was never overly soft in his encouraging comments. It was funny, this young lad schooling me on getting 'er done. But I assured him that would not happen, using his remark to inspire me as the three-week course began.[1] I left the next day for Ottawa, to visit my family and girl friend. Taking Monique out on the town, she remarked she was worried about what would happen to me out in Edmonton. I said I really did not know either, but it was my job to take the next move in my career. I said there was no option for failure, this was a must have or I would face harsh consequences. To fail Basic Para would probably lead to me being RTU'd (kicked out of Airborne).

But I said I was ready for this, I had passed Selection for the past four months. I was in the best shape of my life. This was totally new though, my first trip to Edmonton. I knew that soldiers as proficient or better than me had failed previously. It would not be a cake walk, as the Airborne had informed me already. The instructors mission was to make it a challenge, for the para qualified people they passed would face tougher challenges ahead. Here I thought I had an advantage over the average parachutist recruit. I had seen the Airborne, posted to 3 Commando that summer. I had honed my body, attuned to the daily PT, long runs and tough, timed

---

1 During this time Oct. 23, the US Navy Seals fought in their first action since Vietnam, in Panama. Reference HISTORY NAVY SEALS The Covert Missions of the Military's Elite Fighting Force

marches in hot, humid, dusty roads of Petawawa. Also by now, I actually wanted to be there. This makes it much easier to take the pain, to meet our officer and NCO's lofty expectations. Any soldier or professional who must perform in demanding, dangerous environments knows this. Most take pride in knowing they are performing a job few could or would want to do. Some of them do it for personal glory, some for the pay and prestige. Some for peer pressure or family history in serving one's country. I was in it at first at least, simply because the Army asked me to fill a spot on the Airborne roster.

So, after reassuring my loved ones in Ottawa that weekend, I knew the challenge would be to meet everyone's expectations. Also, adding an incentive, was Mike my older brother, who had passed the course around 1976. We always had a healthy respect and competition going since we were growing up on the farm near Ottawa. He had gone to Germany first before me, leading to my posting there in 1979. Then our career paths diverged, he joining the RCMP, while I went to Carleton University, while serving in the Army Reserve. Then the big change, direct entry into the Regular Force in 1983. That day in November I took a last look at Ottawa, boarding the flight for Edmonton, leaving Uplands Airport for this huge course. As I sat in the seat I knew, or thought that I could be a corpse in a few days. I shrugged it off, closing my eyes as I focussed on positive things. I pictured an Airborne officer pinning the wings on my chest.

Basic Para

November 15, 1983: I arrived in Edmonton that day, my first ever trip to Alberta. It was also my first trip in a Hercules C-130, which would soon be my taxi in the 'Borne. Walking off the rear ramp with about 50 other jump recruits, I slung the duffle bag over my shoulder and jumped onto the tarmac at CFB Namao, the base north of Edmonton. It was sort of like the war flick Platoon, when Charlie Sheen arrived in Vietnam for his tour of duty, except it was cold and bleak, the start of winter. I stood with the gaggle of course trainees as a couple of veteran Airborne Instructors in camouflage SSF smocks and maroon berets arrived to greet us.

As I listened to these veteran Airborne instructors, it was a sort of surreal moment. I was 25 years old, in the prime of my life then. It was a three and a half month journey to get here. I thought of those who had gone before me. The only soldier I knew who had failed their first shot at Basic Para, was strangely enough my first infantry instructor and platoon sergeant, Sergeant MacDonald. He was a legend in my unit, a highly motivated career soldier and in excellent shape. So how did he fail? The others I knew who had been here had passed, starting with my older brother Mike. My buddy Ian Wadleigh advised me to go in with an aggressive attitude, you had to want it! Failure was not an option. I wanted this, I wanted to be tested, to measure myself against the best in the Canadian Army. I felt the pressure knowing that many eyes were on me, I simply had to return to Ontario with my jump wings!

Warrant Officer Robertson, course Senior NCO took our names, then we marched to the base gym across the base. There we changed into PT gear and underwent the preliminary PT test. I had been told at Pre-para that here, most of the failures occurred. It was simple and straight forward, no IQ test as they say. Meet the standard or hit the bricks back home there and then. RTU: returned to unit meant failure. 32 sit-ups, followed by 7 chin-ups and a timed run of 1.5 miles. But we were told they had to be perfect or not counted. An instructor gave us a demo first before we began then we had a minute for each part, the run being about six minutes. I passed it easily, but about half of the recruits failed, vanishing mysteriously never to be seen again! So in a heartbeat the course went from fifty odd to less than thirty. Then the real work began, as we formed up for our first run around the base. We wore combat fatigues, boots and steel helmets, with our name scrawled on the front. This was so our Instructors (we called staff) could take our names at the slightest infraction or failure to meet the course standard. We also had to wear old jump harness strapped tight to our bodies.

As we ran around the base that day at Greisbach, I was in the zone. Having just come through the cauldron of Selection for three months, I was in incredible shape after my wounded feet had heeled. The other recruits, some not having this advantage found it tougher. We lost a few more over the first week, not having the fitness or mental attitude to succeed under the scrutiny of an unsympathetic course staff. After weeding out the chaff, as WO Robertson termed the early failures, the remaining 20 odd recruits went through two weeks of ground training. This included daily runs, with old jump harness strapped to our bodies, rifles and steel helmets. Every mistake cost us 50 push-ups. No walking anywhere, we ran to the eating mess, our barracks, to the staff lounge, ect. Warrant Robertson and the other instructors stated this was not to punish us, but to make us tougher, for paratroopers had to be in top shape.

By the second week, we practiced aircraft drills, landings in the "swings or racks," and notably the famous mock tower. It is still there at CFB Edmonton, decades after the Edmonton Training Center at Greisbach was closed, after the Airborne Regiment was disbanded in

1994. It is about 30 feet high, a mock-up of an aircraft fuselage on wooden struts. It used to stand at Greisbach in North-west Edmonton, probable moved to the main base, now called Steele Barracks. The instructors punished us relentlessly with various torture methods. Apart from hundreds of push-ups, verbal assaults (trying to get inside our heads) there was the Airborne swim. This was banned sometime after my course as being too nasty. Inside the gym, after someone screwed up, the remaining recruits adopted the push-up position, crawling around the track using your arms only! If the guy in front collapsed in fatigue, you were told not to stop, crawl right over the unlucky, gasping recruit.

Others were left over coffee break, dangling from the landing swing harness. It was not good (never happened to me), the unlucky recruit in agony as the harness bit into his groin and shoulders. These simulated landings were the worst part for me. This drill practiced the para trainee in the four basic types of landings. Forward (left/right) and rear (left/right). We stood on a platform, our harness hooked to a rope, secured to an overhead pulley. An instructor held the free end securely as we jumped off, swinging to and fro. At the last second, he would call out one of the prescribed landing type. It was all instinctive as one had seconds to react before landing hard on a floor mat. I cracked my head the first few attempts. Even though we wore steel jump helmets, it was painful. I was not a natural at this but my instructor passed me.

"I don't care if you fuck up and hurt yourself, as long as you don't injure some other guy. Pass Gilligan!" Finally, it was time for the mock tower, the final hurdle before Jump Week.

The trick here was half mental/ half physical as I found out quickly. Not that it was easy. We practiced several exits on the ground before the test began. As you went out the side door, we had to exhibit the airborne exit to perfection, throw the static line forward, pivot left or right, then head down, jump out (called the jab) and clear the fuselage. This is why paratroopers get extra pay and train so hard. It is potentially suicidal, extremely dangerous and life threatening. Failure to clear the aircraft fuselage meant one could get hung up and bounce off the side. We wear told the only way to survive was to be hauled back in by the Herc crew with a retrieval system. I heard one jumper had his static line cut, plummeted to his death, due to being knocked out and unable to deploy his reserve. As you fall to earth, if you have not shut your eyes, you see yourself plummeting down face first to your untimely death or injury. This is the so-called moment of truth, where many quit. Then the static line, fixed to your harness and an overhead cable arrests your fall sharply. The gasping recruit then zips down the angled cable (death slide) to land on a slope about 100 meters away.

It was exacting and zero room for error, the staff demanded perfection. We had to do several good exits, one out each side, one with a rifle only, one with full equipment. In the end, I passed, while I believe there was only one failure. Surprisingly a Major refused to go, until then he was breezing through the course. The survivors, around twenty by now, were ecstatic as we had passed the rigors of the two-week ground training. There were two possibilities left: victory or death! During Jump week, we had to perform a minimum of six parachute descents without getting hurt. But that Friday night, we celebrated at a local Edmonton bar known as a Borne hangout, just off base. This was The Rosslyn Inn Pub, located on 137 Avenue and 97th Street in North West Edmonton, on the south edge of Greisbach Airborne Training Center. It is still there today, three decades later, though Greisbach is now a residential part of the city. I bought a maroon t-shirt for the occasion, with the wings displayed on front. My group of jump trainees walked in, with ZZ Top blaring from the sound system and ordered a round of drinks. It was packed in The Roz as we partied at the bar, with a few Indians sitting nearby. I heard them challenge us with an "Airborne sucks" taunt. I stood up before a huge Indian, but was replaced by one of my instructors. He smiled and said sit down, enjoy your night trooper. I did and watched as he quickly demolished the Indian in a flurry of left and rights. It was a wild night.

November 29: I sat inside the hangar, dressed in jump rig and gear, waiting for my first ever parachute jump. I was jacked as my load of twelve recruits (stick) sat on the bench. Then nearing jump hour, we head the hated words "Stop drop." There was about an hour delay, then we heard one of the recruits had broken his leg and/or back on landing. The instructors stood glaring down at us. "What did we tell you about trying to stand on landing?"

"Do not stand Staff!" A dozen lungs roared back. WO Robertson grimacing, told us what was happening next. After the injured recruit was medevacked to the hospital, thus failing the course, we would perform our jump. It was an administrative or non-tactical jump with no equipment. I was slotted in at #6 starboard side on the C-130. We would jump over DZ Buxton, just to the north. We were told later it was named after the former RSM of the Airborne, after he had 'thundered in' at the DZ years before. This was a bit unnerving. For if God (any RSM) could die, why not an insignificant jump recruit like me? Armed with this information, we proceeded out of the hangar for the short walk to the waiting, lumbering hulk of the Hercules transport. My life and world were about to undergo rapid change for an eternity!

We walked up the rear ramp, filing into our assigned seats and sat down. Strapped into my CT-1 harness I leaned back on the nylon seat, trying to relax. It all happened quick, the ramp came up, we buckled in and the C-130 roared down the runway. It hit me then, this was it, another hurdle to get over. Before I knew it, we had reached jump altitude. The Jump Master ordered us to stand and hook up. After checking our equipment, we received the final check by our JM. It was not a full load in the Herc, so there was plenty of room. Also, it was "bare assed" meaning we had no equipment loading us down. It was the easiest jump I would ever do. The JM passes on final data from the Herc crew chief, wind strength and altitude, about 1200 feet.

I held on to the static line as I stood behind five other recruits on the starboard (right side) as the pilot slowed the aircraft to jump speed as we neared DZ Buxton. The crew chief opened the doors and inspected the exits. He might have tossed out a WDI (wind drift indicator) which the DZ ground crew used to make final corrections for the plane's approach. This is done because the worst jump in Canadian history had occurred on May 8, 1968 when 26 paratroopers jumping on the Mattawa Plain had been blown into the Ottawa River. At least seven paras (Signallers and 1 RCR) had drowned before the safety boat got to them.[2]

"Who are you?" The JM's yelled above the noise. "Airborne!" Sixteen throats roared back. "One minute! Standby." I saw the red light blink on beside the jump

---

2   Into Icy Waters: by Tom MacGregor; Pg. 48-52; **LEGION MAGAZINE MAY/JUNE 2018 LEGIONMAGAZINE.COM; Publisher: Canvet Publications Ltd.**

door. Adrenaline pulsed through my veins as I focussed on the next action I would take. I flexed my muscles, my hand checking helmet straps again, my right arm swaying back and forth to ensure the static line road smoothly on the overhead cable. Then the green light flicked on, "GO! Go! Go!"

The JM's had already positioned the number 1 in the door, so he simply jumped off. In seconds, I reached the door, threw the static line forward, pivoted into the door, my hands touching the sides, then I jabbed out into the wintry world outside. My hands gripped the belly reserve, my heels clicked together and my chin pressed down on my chest. I counted to four as my body was whipped sideways by the prop blast, the big engine feet away. I don't remember but I probably closed my eyes, for the next thing I knew was the jerk on the rig straps as the CT-1 canopy cracked open above me. I looked up and checked the canopy as it fluttered then filled, cracking fully open, a beautiful sight to a new jumper. "Whoo! Hell ya! I'm alive!"

It was a big round canopy, hooking my body to a set of four main risers. I heard the Herc flying away, six more jumpers exiting from both sides. I was jubilant and let out a shout of joy. My hands gripped the risers as I went through the flight drills, looking down at the snow covered DZ Buxton a thousand feet below my boots. I saw jumpers descending all around me, but no one was close. So, I focussed on the landing, looking for the wind indicator. It is important to point into any breeze, as this controls and slows the chute. Unlike modern civilian high performance elliptical chutes, my CT-1 had no toggle lines and is slow to turn. I gripped the risers and tugged to make a last adjustment as I got lower. It was early winter and below zero but I barely noticed. The adrenaline still screamed through my veins and I was in the zone. Satisfied I would hit a safe area with no obstacles, I assumed the landing position, feet and knees together, slightly bent, hands gripping the overhead risers, chin tucked into chest.

"Left front roll, relax," I thought as I saw my drift with the ground now rising rapidly. I hit with my boots digging into the snow-covered ground, grunting from the impact and rolled. I did my first perfect roll ever, then standing up I brushed the snow off my uniform. I gave the thumbs up to some ground crew nearby then let out a whoop of joy. I had done my first jump and survived without a scratch. The tension and nervous fear vanished, replaced by a sort of wave of euphoria. Only jumpers can know this feeling after a first jump or a successful big jump. I had reached a new level in my life, never to look back on what I had been. The same day I jumped with a rifle attached to my shoulder. This was an AE- Administrative equipment jump, and I moved to Number 3, Port side. The jump went to plan, until the final part, where I released the waist band securing my old stripped down rifle. I released the rifle off my shoulder and dropped it at about 30-feet above ground. It was fixed to a cord to drop about 15 feet. I assumed the landing position, thumping into the snow easily and rolled. I got up gasping and gave the thumbs up to an instructor and some other jumpers as they landed several meters away. Then I packed my big chute up, looking for my rifle, which should have been right there.

"Ooops!" I saw it about 20 odd feet away, buried barrel first into the dirt. I casually walked over to it, gripped the butt and wrenched it free, dusting the snow off. As I said it was non-operational, used only for these training jumps. I saw the wooden fore stock was cracked from the hard landing. I wrapped the cord around it then nonchalantly walked back to the pick-up vehicle. I dumped my gear into a pile, then mingled with the rest of the trainees. I never heard anything about it, the instructor even complimented me on my excellent canopy control and landing. This surprised me, as I had noted in the 'Borne, compliments for lower ranks were exceptionally few and far between. When one passed a course or task, no one said anything, unless one screwed the pooch. Otherwise it was on to the next task at hand, in this case my third and full equipment jump on Day 1 of Jump week. The Course jumpers were issued with a Parachute Jump Record, a small blue book, in which all our jumps were recorded, signed off by an official. In this case WO Robertson, the course Senior NCO signed off all Basic Para jumps.

I still have this, my first jump record book. Later, when I became a civilian skydiver, I used jump books to record all jumps, used by CSPA as one progressed in advancing, attaining licenses and ratings. At present, I have close to 500 civilian skydives (most freefall) and 50 Army static line jumps. As Jump week progressed, back in November 1983, my primary concern was keeping healthy. If we were injured during Jump week, we could return later to complete the required jumps without a black mark, but for me this was not acceptable. Most of ground training was done. We still did morning runs as time permitted, but were easy compared with the first two weeks. The Instructor staff eased things a bit, encouraging us to complete the requirements for passing, becoming trained paratroopers and an asset to the Airborne Regiment. I was constantly shifted around in position for each jump, so I experienced how these changes affected one's performance. I did my third jump that day, November 29, at number 15 Starboard side. This being full equipment, a rucksack was attached by two quick release clips, dangling over my legs and rigged with a retainer rope to my harness.

Unlike when I jumped with the regiment later, this ruck was light, packed with newspaper. I also carried a mock rifle on my shoulder as before. Dressed in winter gear we walked out to the waiting Hercules and boarded. It went smooth as we got more accustomed to the routine. All the trainees were in high spirits at this point, as we could see the light at the end of the tunnel. With each jump, I gained confidence, with more knowledge I relied on my training and the professional attitude of the JM instructors and Herc crew. Also, the para riggers who packed our chutes, so far there had been no malfunctions on opening. Half an hour later I exited the Herc, noticing how the noise diminished as the plane flew away. I was left alone, swaying slowly from the CT-1 chute, enjoying the scenery as I drifted down to DZ Buxton. I looked around at mother Earth below, then the city skyline to the south. What a view I thought excitedly… and I am being paid to see this! I embraced this moment, just me and the world! At about 500 feet, I released the waist band, holding the rifle by the sling as I hit the quick releases under the belly reserve. The rifle and rucksack dropped and dangled below me from the nylon cord as the ground rose about 200 feet below. I kicked the line, so the load swayed to and fro, then assumed the landing position. I heard the equipment load hit the ground, then seconds after I thudded onto the ground and rolled. I got up and cracked a grin as another trooper landed nearby. After gathering our gear, we trotted off the DZ high fiving each other.

"Awesome eh dude? Soon we will have our wings!" Power was a buddy from 8th CH, Recce Squadron, based at Petawawa and part of SSF. He was one of the first tankers to get his wings, as future drops would drop some Lynx armoured vehicles with the Airborne Battle

Group, to be used as reconnaissance and armour support to the ground troops. Later after all the jumpers returned to the hangar, WO Robertson debriefed us. We had completed three jumps that day, three to go, the last being the Grad jump. After turning in our jump gear, we were dismissed late that afternoon. Running back to barracks, we hurriedly stripped for showers, then dressed in civilian clothes we hit the eating mess, then the town to celebrate. Edmonton once the home of the Airborne, still recognized 'Borne soldiers, sporting maroon t-shirts as we bar hopped, starting with The Rosslyn Inn. We sampled Edmonton's night life, downing a few beers, our small group exchanged stories of our jump experiences. But primarily we looked ahead to the next day and finishing the deal. Later in barracks, I lay awake, dreaming of the wings being pinned on my chest and handed the maroon beret and Airborne cap badge.

Next day, November 30, the daily routine continued. Reveille and morning run, shower, dress, the eating mess, then report to the hangar at the air field. For this fourth jump, I was again #15 Starboard, full equipment, but this time off the C-130 rear ramp. This was a new experience, but we practiced it beforehand in mock-ups during ground training and a refresher in the hangar. It turned out to be less stressful and easier than the side door. It also gave us a panoramic view of the world outside, after the big rear ramp was lowered. After reaching jump altitude, we stood up and did equipment checks, receiving the final JM check. All good, he gave us the thumbs up, then yelled "Standby. One minute." The starboard stick followed the port stick to the ramp, holding the static line over our helmets, clipped to the overhead cable.

I heard "Go! Go! Go!" My eyes were glued to the jump light on the fuselage as it flicked from red to green. The feeling I got stayed with me for years, a feeling of upcoming excitement and adrenaline rush. I watched as one by one, the jumpers ahead flung the static line, then ran off the ramp. As I shuffled forward, I watched for the first time, as the camouflage green chutes billowed open, a line of chutes stretched away before me. It was the biggest drop yet, then I was there…poised on the edge of the ramp. I hesitated for a split second, drinking in the moment, then jabbed off the ramp into space. There was no prop blast this time, as I fell away, looking straight down at the ground below. Everything seemed to slow down a bit, as mentally my mind picked up speed. The chute jerked open above after four seconds, then I drifted after the long line of chutes ahead. We yelled at each other, as the DZ landing approached about 1000 feet below. It was important to observe everything around one, not get distracted by the excitement of the moment. In the end, this was a job, practice for the bigger, more challenging mass drops ahead. Loaded down with heavy loads, mostly at night, in all kinds of weather and terrain. But for now, I enjoyed the moment and landed shortly after without complications.

The second jump that day, my 5th was another ramp jump, but with no equipment. It was needless to say, Captain Obvious, a piece of cake. Again, I was #15 Starboard, so it went like clock work. We were coming together as a team as we yelled out chants of 'Airborne', whooping and patting each other as we ran toward the waiting ramp, hurtling our bodies into the late autumn air outside. Going off the ramp, I learned the exit was all about momentum, speed and team work. You followed the jumper ahead and one eye on the jump light and JM. He was watching for hang-ups and other problems, so if he held up his hand before you, you stopped. So, it was not all fun and games. This was serious shit and one wrong move could dump one into a serious problem. But again, I landed safely on DZ Buxton and lived.

I knew something of the history of military parachuting. It all began in WW2 when German parachutists jumped into Holland as part of Blitzkrieg. For Canada, we followed the British and Americans in responding with our first parachute unit, the 1st Canadian Parachute Battalion. Formed in June 1942, the recruits were taken from regular combat units, then trained in England at Ringway, Cheshire, home of the Parachute Training School by the RAF.

The cadre of trained parachutists (paras) returned to Canada, then subsequently shipped/trained to Fort

Benning, Georgia to continue training. At that early stage, Canada had no bases for parachute training. Later during the war, the first was established at Shilo, Manitoba in 1943. The first jump aircraft included the Lockheed Loadstar which carried 10 jumpers in one stick. The British used the Albemarle bomber, exiting from a hole cut in the floor. These were used to drop spies into Occupied France, Eastern Europe and Norway to work with Underground Resistance fighters. The mainstay of Allied Airborne units during the war was the American built DAK or C-47 Douglas Dakota which carried 18 jumpers. They were also used to tow gliders, which were used in combat jumps, later in Holland in September 1944.

The German Falchirmjagger had first landed gliders in 1940, landing a handpicked team of paratroopers in a surprise attack on the roof of Belgian fortress of Eben Emael. The 1st Canadian Parachute Battalion's first CO, Major H.D. Proctor was killed on his first jump in Fort Benning. It is believed the unlucky jumper collided with another jump aircraft, entangling his chute and killed instantly. There was also the 2nd Canadian Parachute Battalion raised in 1942, subsequently becoming integrated into the new joint US-Canadian 1st Special Service Force, nicknamed The Devil's Brigade by the Germans while fighting in Sicily and Italy (1943-44).

Finally, on December 1st, Graduation Day arrived. My 6th jump was to be a AEN (Administrative Night jump with equipment). It was a long wait, as I sat on the hangar bench, dressed in full equipment. I was not a smoker at that time, so spent the long wait sort of drifting in and out of sleep. As things got going, we heard the ominous "stop drop" once more. Again, one of our recruit mates had been injured. WO Robertson warned us not to take this final jump lightly. "All of you who make the jump will pass and receive your wings. Tomorrow their will be a final "bonus jump" out of a Twin Otter. Then Wings parade and back to your home base. Airborne!" We roared back in response, as we awaited our final jump.

    The worst part for me was that final period of waiting, for now I was starting to sweat in the warm hangar in full gear. We finally got the go ahead, standing and stretching, adjusting our gear, then the JM's checked us out, ensuring all straps were tight, pin checks and such. Then we waddled out the door to the waiting Hercules in the pitch blackness of early December. For this jump I was slotted into #2 Starboard. I liked this spot I found out, standing behind the stick leader, with a great view outside the door. Shortly after taking off, we began the drills for exit. It was becoming routine for me by now, but I focussed on staying cool headed, going over my aircraft, exit, in air and landing procedures. At last, the red light turned green and the lead jumper in the door exited. I followed, throwing my static line, squared off in the door, then exited with a strong jab into the dark murkiness of the night. My chute cracked open, jerking me back to the land of the living. I was calm as I descended slowly in the night air, seeing the brightly lit city of Edmonton off to the south. After releasing my equipment, I landed on the frozen ground of the DZ. I crawled to my feet, nodding to a nearby jumper.

After dumping our gear at the waiting truck, I bummed a cigarette from one of my mates, enjoying that first smoke in a state of euphoria. After months of Selection, I was now a qualified Canadian paratrooper! That night we celebrated in the Junior Ranks drinking mess. I got hammered for the first time since arriving in Edmonton three weeks before. Of course, I had a hangover the next morning, but who cared? Our final jump next day was a bare assed fun jump from a Twin Otter. This was a smaller twin engine turbo prop, used for many purposes as it was STOL (short take-off & landing), it could land on makeshift landing strips in the high Arctic, search and rescue or long distance chartered flights, not to mention parachuting.

Later in my life, after my career tour in the Canadian Forces ended, I would do many more skydives from a Twin Otter, along with many other fixed wing aircraft and helicopters. More on this later, but on December 2 I boarded the Twin Otter as #5. There was only one door, therefore a single stick of paras crammed inside, but there was a bench to sit on. It was a fast, short ride to the top as we relaxed on the bench, devoid of equipment, just our jump rig and helmets. We jumped a bit higher for this administrative fun jump, around 2000 feet. It was static line and the opening was softer, as the plane could slow down more than the Herc.

We were in a great mood, laughing and joking with the JM and pilots. "This is luxury!" I shouted as we lined up for the exit. Thus, it was a fun jump as I floated down to DZ Buxton for the final time in my life. It would also be my only jump from a Twin Otter as a paratrooper, the bulk being from the Hercules, the 'Borne's preferred taxi into battle. It went smoothly, but I did not dismiss or take lightly the landing, rolling as before. Then back at the hangar, we formed up for Wings parade. On December 2 the course officer, Captain Neale pinned the wings on my chest, going down the line of grads, about 20 of us, shaking our hands, then we saluted.

The course and Jump week were completed ahead of time, so we had a few days to enjoy Edmonton before the flight back to our home bases. Little did I know, I would return to Edmonton many times, eventually settling down in the northern Alberta capital decades later in 2002. Coincidentally I bought my first house on the edge of Griesbach, after it was disbanded.

Also as well as being home base, I would do hundreds of jumps in Alberta and across the planet, most being civilian freefall. After our short celebratory leave, most of us newly minted paratroopers arrived back in Petawawa. I returned to 10 Platoon, now wearing the maroon beret and Airborne cap badge for the first time. However, as I soon found, I was not a fully-fledged para and Selection continued. I returned triumphantly however, my platoon mates and family heaping praise on me after my three-week absence. Major Leavy the CO of 3 Commando had me report into his office for a short talk. I returned to earth quickly, as the Bear looked up at me, squeezing his hand exercise grip (maybe it was a ball), I barely remember. At any rate, he didn't offer me a congratulatory bear hug, nor a drink.

"Gilligan, do you know why you are here?" He was staring at me with that grim look.

"No Sir." I responded, looking down at a thick file on his desk. It turned out it was a report from the Military Police. It concerned my last job before joining the Airborne. I was a staff instructor or Umpire, tasked with inducting new Reserve Officer Cadets into the Armed Forces. A couple of the Cadets had complained about the rough treatment by the course staff. I heard this before, basic whining by rich, spoiled brats. I told the CO that, I followed the rules, following the Course Senior NCO's direction. One guy showed up at the course, for the early morning run dressed in a civilian suit. This officer cadet was in my section, the first thing being early morning PT. I asked the Course Warrant Officer what to do with him. He said run him with the rest in whatever he was wearing. I smiled and nodded. He ran in his suit, falling out after a short stretch of maybe a 100 meters. Later he dropped his FN rifle while on parade doing drill. He was given standard extra drill, running around the parade square with his FN rifle over his head. His father claimed I had abused him and had the MP's conduct a thorough investigation.

Major Leavy told me this, but added he would not press any charges. He congratulated me on my successful Basic Para course and Selection so far. But added my time in the Borne was just beginning. In January, Winter Warfare would start and full equipment night jumps.

"OK Trooper Gilligan. If you want to command men here, respect them, do not abuse your authority. I will have my eye on you. I demand Airborne standards are met. Dismissed."

Winter/Arctic Warfare Training

After my return to Petawawa, in the first week of December, my unit 3 Commando transitioned quickly into Winter Warfare mode. At this point, I was a no name Para recruit basically. It was complex and confusing, over the next four months I participated in several ops. To be considered a fully trained Airborne soldier, I had to qualify in a blistering array of skills, at the end of which I was raised to the level of TQ4 Infantryman (trade 031). In some cases, I had already performed allot of these tasks (e.g. Ceremonial drill). I had been a section commander as a member of Ceremonial Guard in Ottawa. I was temporarily assigned to one of the Reserve Regiments (Governor General Foot Guards), trained, instructed and participated in mounting guard at Parliament Hill and the GG's official mansion. I have five pages of qualifications in my personal records, just for this level. In some cases my quals were ignored, I repeated the Basic Infantry Comms course and the Machine gun course (a waste of time in my opinion), as I could have taught the courses! My objection was ignored and I did the courses and passed them easily, trying not to doze off. Of these Machine guns were of great interest to me and they became my specialty. I knew them intimately, both our Canadian types (7.62 mm GPMG and Heavy mg M2 .50 Cal), as well as our Allies (US M-60) and our enemy (USSR).

In 3 Commando, Basic Winter Warfare training commenced, to get us new guys on the same page as the rest of the 'Borne. Back then, the Regiment and its Officers were given allot of latitude to run the Regiment as they saw fit. Outsiders like myself were not trusted until one proved beyond a shadow of a doubt that you deserved to be there and wanted it! Later on this would change, leading to the problems occurred in Somalia in the 90's. I was told that I was on a sort of probationary period until June 1984. By that time, the powers that be (my OC Major Leavy) would decide my future. In December then, my platoon did training separate from the rest of the company and regiment. It was basic stuff, using Arctic gear, care and maintenance of weapons in an austere environment, avoiding frostbite, towing section sleds, erecting the Arctic section tent in any conditions day or night, night patrols, navigation, et.

This led to the first field exercise that winter, Ex. Pegasus Strike, which ran from December 5-12. M/Cpl Miles was my section commander in 10 Platoon. My job as a C-2 gunner was to participate in all tasks assigned to us, display ability to acquire and retain knowledge, be self-motivated, show leadership qualities (even though I was given no power), in other words excel at any given task and strive to be a super-soldier. I found it at bit frustrating at the time but I did my job. Any compliments for a job well done went to my superiors, along with promotion and other trinkets. I remember endless marches loaded down with allot of gear and pulling loaded toboggans to bivouac sites in the woods. The last part I remember well, Winter survival for a week in the depths of a cold, snow covered woods. 10 Platoon were on our own for this, supervised by our Sergeant McClean. We went without the arctic tent, lantern and stove. Instead we used axes to chop down trees and built a lean-to shelter. The first night we built a fire pit in front of the lean-to to keep from freezing to death. We used layers of fir branches to sleep on, as we also were forbidden from using our sleeping bags or air mattresses.

This did not go down well with some of the soldiers. "WTF are we hauling all of this equipment around for Sarge? We busted our butts for miles to get here, hauling that crap, then we don't used it! We have no rations, no coffee, what gives?" The Sergeant shook his head at us as we stood around the fire, trying to keep warm. "You guys are Airborne now. What do you expect, everything handed to you? Maid service maybe? Tomorrow you will learn to survive off the land. We will build snares and traps, then go fishing. All of you have survival gear, right? Fishing line, jump knives and a pack of matches. All yer need to survive out here."

We were organized for the night into fire watch shifts. The task here was keep the fire stocked, guard the platoon area and awake the next relief. The next morning, we found that we had indeed survived the first night in the frosty, wintry wood. However one man, Trooper Gravel from North Bay had an unfortunate accident. While on fire watch, he took off his mukluk foot wear to thaw out by the fire. He had then dozed off for a few minutes I guess, for his mukluks as he showed the Sergeant were a twisted, blackened wreck of burnt rubber and nylon. We chuckled at his misfortune, several jokes made the rounds as the Sarge smiled at a crestfallen Gravel. The young trooper suggested he be medivacked back to base, as he was now in sock feet in -20C something and the middle of nowhere. Instead the cunning senior NCO handed him two plastic bags. "Here ya go Trooper Gravel. Your new winter boots!"

As Gravel looked on stunned, we broke into hysterical laughter. As he pulled the plastic bags on his feet, we passed cigarettes around and lit up. Our morale thus restored, we got down to business. We broke into small groups, one to gather more fire wood, a few to set traps and some to find a fishing spot and catch us dinner. For any fans of the series SURVIVOR, this was no tropical island paradise, with attached film crew and playing silly games. If we did not catch our food we starved. But thanks to the snow and ice, water was not a problem. We had a large pressure cooker from the toboggan, which we used to melt snow and cook rations. Over that week, our platoon survived, even flourishing in the wintry wilderness. We caught several fish, collected berries and even snagged a couple of bunny rabbits. As well as a fowl or two.

Slowly this bunch of forlorn ragamuffins transformed into the unit which would eventually become one of the best I ever served with. We emerged a week later not losing a single man to injury or frostbite. I was an accepted member of the platoon now, at least by my platoon mates. Finally back at base, around mid December, we cleaned our gear and ourselves, taking our first shave and shower in over a week. As the famous Lord Wellington once said, "I don't know if my soldiers will frighten the French. But they put the fear of God in me!"

The 'Borne on field tactical exercise dispensed with all normal routine. No use of soap, razors, bathing or scented after shave. Slowly we became animals, blending into the natural environment, to become the best winter warfare soldiers on the planet, our primary mission being protection of the Canadian Arctic from foreign interlopers. 2 Para our British counterparts, 2nd

Battalion of the British Parachute Regiment, who trained with us in Norway on winter exercises where also noted to be proficient, almost at our level. We exchanged a few picked officers with the Parachute Regiment to learn each other's methods and expertise.

Our 12 Platoon at that time was run by a British officer, a Captain Fisher. When I was transferred to 12 Platoon later, I found the Captain marched at a quite fast pace, as we did, calling it the 'Borne shuffle. It was speed marching, faster than other "leg battalions." One of the annual quals for Combat Arms soldiers was the 2x10 miler. For regular infantry battalions, it was a ten-mile march on back to back days, carrying weapons and full fighting order, under two hours. For most Airborne platoons, which was the size of unit the march was performed, the time was under 1.5 hours. Later the Army dispensed with this qualification.

So as Christmas approached, we finished cleaning and storing our winter gear and weapons in the Commando Storage lock-ups. Then somewhat reluctantly, our leaders cut us loose for two weeks Holiday leave. At this point, I still had no personal vehicle, so my older brother Mike picked me up for the drive to Ottawa and home. I felt jubilant as I arrived back in Ottawa, after surviving six months of Airborne Selection. It was relaxing, getting re-acquainted with the world, my family and friends. During the two weeks, my mind was focussed on what was next in my military adventures. I was informed that on return in January, the Regiment would gear up for Winter Warfare, including two major tactical parachute mass drops, somewhere in Northern Ontario. So I kept up my physical training even during holidays.

It was a meat grinder, as I found out over the next few months. It was meant to be challenging, those who did not meet the standard were gone by the next summer. As well over my stay in the 'Borne, every year there was up to a 30% change over, as personnel were posted out to other army units, remustered to different trades or released from the Forces altogether. Others went on long courses, such as the Pathfinder Recce Course (6 months), Jump Master, Mountain school instructor, American Ranger course and others. Every year, usually late summer, Airborne ran Jump Bivouac, welcoming our Allied brothers. Returning paras also got reacquainted, doing the odd jump and telling stories. Picked soldiers were likewise sent to other foreign airborne units to attain their wings. These included the British Parachute Regiment, German Falchirmjagger, French Foreign Legion, French Commandos, American 82nd Airborne Division in Fort Bragg, NC. But for me, it was the grinding Winter Warfare exercises.

January 3, 1984: Early that Monday morning, 3 Commando paraded on the square dressed for a run. It was bitterly cold as the Platoon Sergeants took our names. Major Leavy kept the same routine as before in warmer weather. Dressed in light PT gear, I froze in the icy air as we jogged down the road. A light mist rose above the ground eerily, several troopers still hung over, got sick and vomited as we ran along. It was short, around 4 miles, after finishing it was a sprint to the barracks to thaw out under hot showers. Also that week, we had to pass a timed four miler, a pass being under 32 minutes. I averaged around 26 minutes, so apart from freezing my balls off (almost) it was no big deal. Now, we were preparing for the next big deal, the first winter Ex. Several members of the Commando were chosen to go to Trenton, to assist in rigging the heavy loads, our toboggans were to be dropped off the Herc ramps on pallets.

Also our vehicles and snowmobiles would go off the ramps. Individually we packed our rucksacks, including rations, extra ammo, MG belts and mortar rounds, then rigged them for the jump. It was slated for January 20, during meetings we were briefed on the plan. The Regiment was to parachute onto Round Lake, north-east of Petawawa. It was a night, equipment tactical jump (TEN), the first I would be tasked with the Regiment. After landing, the tough work began. I had a bet with the Platoon 2 I/C, PB (Panic button) McClean, who wagered that I would not survive it. I laughed at him, for although I was a fairly new guy in the 'Borne, I was not new to Winter Warfare. I knew I was under a magnifying glass, the Airborne did things a bit different. Again, I used negative comments made by my Platoon sergeant, to motivate me. I don't know if I call it hate, but as we approached the jump date, I was extremely motivated to prove the sergeant wrong.

Ex. Pegasus Blizzard: Finally on January 20, all preparations made, the Regiment was relocated to the Airhead at Trenton, Ontario. We received final briefings, the DZ was called Chevrolet, the frozen Round Lake. By now the Pathfinder Platoon had already jumped in and were testing the ice for safety reasons, assisted by our Engineer Squadron. They also monitored the weather and winds. By evening we were told it was a go. It was exciting being a small part of this Regimental winter jump. Somewhere around 750 paratroopers scurried around the hangars as we got dressed for the jump. Outside on the taxi runways, some 24 Hercules C-130's also got ready, going through pre-flight checks. Last thing was to hit the head, as it would be the last chance for days. Groups of jumpers went outside, for a last smoke and a chat. Sometime after midnight, long sticks of loaded down paratroopers waddled out of the hangars and made our way for the waiting C-130's. We wore full winter clothes, with white cam being the last layer. I felt my heart beating in excitement, for in a few hours I would lose my cherry, as the vets called a new jumper. Everybody new it, as I was reminded of several times.

My platoon was pretty tightly knit by now, so they sheltered me somewhat, nodding at me and adding their encouragement. It was simple to me, rely on your training, your mates and the equipment. Focus in the present, not some hypothetical future, in which anything could happen. As I finally plunked down on the Herc seat, I went over mentally the drills I had been taught in Edmonton, a little over a month before. I was #2 Port side door for this jump.

For these tactical night jumps, typically the guy with the heaviest load went first. So the stick leader was the machine gunner, a small guy named Eaton. His load was so heavy, it weighed more than he did, so we had to help him stand. I have even seen the MG gunner sit in the door, then the JM kicked or shoved him out! I stood behind him, as we did equipment checks, the plane bucking violently in turbulent air as it descended below a thousand feet.

It was January 20, 1984 as I sat in the C-130 Hercules transport. It had been a long, noisy flight from the airhead at CFB Trenton, where The Canadian Airborne Regiment had boarded the 24 Hercules several hours earlier. For myself, Trooper Sean Gilligan, I was assigned to 10 Platoon, 3 Commando, a company sized unit of the regiment, one of three infantry companies, mostly recruited from the three Regular battalions of The Canadian Armed Forces. My unit, 3 Commando comprised about 150 men, mostly recruited from the three battalions of the Royal Canadian Regiment. 1 Commando similarly was composed of members of the Royal 22nd Regiment from Quebec. 2 Commando was allied to the PPCLI, whose three battalions were based in Western Canada. Other units jumping that night were Service Commando (drivers, support elements), HQ & Signals Squadron, gunners from E Battery, RCHA, RC Engineers and troopers from the new Recce Squadron, 8th C.H.,[3] attached to the Airborne Battle Group, the nucleus of Canada's Special Service Force, the quick reaction element of the Canadian Army.

Inside the rear fuselage of the transport plane, I was squeezed in beside a row of other paratroopers. I was number 2, port side, loaded down like the others with a ton of gear. The dimly lit interior was noisy from the four huge engines, their blades slicing through the freezing air above Northern Ontario. As we approached the Drop Zone, DZ Chevy, which was Round Lake, a frozen lake north of CFB Petawawa, our home base, I peered at my watch's luminous face excitedly. It was after midnight as I glanced out the side windows in the fuselage. The plane was rocking, like a ship in a storm. Despite the cool temperatures, I was starting to sweat.

Dressed in Arctic gear for this exercise, my first winter ex and tactical jump with the regiment (TEN), I was strapped into a CT-1 harness. This secured the main CT-1 parachute to my back and reserve to my belly. Also, strapped on my right shoulder was my personal weapon,

---

[3] 8th C.H. (Canadian Hussars: Armoured Regiment based in CFB Petawawa in 1980's. The first paratroopers from the Armour were on my Basic Para and jumped at Round Lake the next month.

a FN C-2 automatic rifle. My rucksack hung from two quick release mechanisms attached to my parachute harness. I also wore combat fighting gear, holding six rifle magazines (30 round 7.62 mm), two canteens, bayonet, gas mask and grenade pouch. In my rucksack was packed around 200 spare rounds for the C-2, two spare mortar rounds, smoke grenades, flares and cigarettes.

Also, I carried two weeks' rations, spare clothing, socks and sleeping bag. Altogether well over 100 pounds, which pressed my body into the nylon seat. Thankfully unlike some others, I did not experience air sickness. We could get "puke bags," if we felt the urge to relieve our churning guts. I closed my eyes as the Hercules droned in the moonlit sky approaching the DZ. It had been a long, torturous, demanding journey to get to this point. I had joined the Canadian Army eight years earlier. Finally, I was posted to The Canadian Airborne in June 1983, about six months earlier. I received the coveted silver wings and maroon beret after passing my Basic Parachutist Course (8317) last December 2, 1983 at Canadian Airborne Center, Edmonton. Then I heard the expected command from the Jump Master.

"Look this way! Stand up!" I felt an immediate sense of relief, for one thing I always hated was waiting. I released the seat belt and grunting heaved myself to my feet. The plane lurched as the fourty odd paratroopers did the same. The Herc fuselage now became a buzz of noisy, frantic activity as we prepared for the upcoming parachute jump into the icy cold blackness that awaited us. My mind went back to the drills I was taught two months earlier during the three weeks of Basic Para. I adjusted the steel jump helmet on my head, fastening the two straps securely.

"OK buddy here we freaking go!" I thought silently, taking the static line from my reserve and adjusting the hold (fold or bite), then staring intently at the JM a few yards away.

"Hook up!" Sergeant Rockheim yelled, making a two-handed gesture, like some oversized airline stewardess! I clicked the metal fastener to the overhead cable on my left, then jerked on it to ensure it was fastened securely. JM Rockheim gave us the thumbs up and gave the next command, "Check your equipment!" As we did this, the two JM's made their way down the line to check everything was in order. As this was a tactical training jump, this step would be deleted, if this was a real combat jump. My left hand held the static line, while my right went over my equipment in the practiced routine. After the JM inspected each of us he slapped our back, yelling "Your OK jumper!" I breathed a sigh of relief, for as a new para I tried to avoid a critical mistake. He did adjust my harness straps tighter however, as the opening of the chute rapidly decelerated the body plus attached gear. Another trooper down the stick was not as fortunate. I heard him beaking off to the hulking JM, a critical error in judgement.

Rockheim was not one to be trifled with I will tell you for nothing. His punishment was to be unhooked and strapped down prone on the seats for the return flight to Trenton. Then if lucky, he would repeat the whole process and jump sometime the next day! Things were progressing rapidly now, as after a few minutes the JMs completed their checks and returned to the side doors. They gave the thumbs up to the Herc crew chief who was in communication with the flight crew in the cabin. "Ten minutes! Winds 10!" He smiled at the JMs' as they conversed, cracking insults and jokes at each other. I peered at the door as the red light blinked on. I felt the rush of adrenaline hit me like a fist. Then the JM cracked open the side door and an icy blast hit me like a punch. "WTF am I doing here? I'm not fucking doing..."

I watched the JM check the side door for obstructions, then hit the floor and lean outside for a look. As Number 2, I had a front-seat view of the black hell outside, a few winking lights below, something like 800 feet. My back and muscles were starting to ache by now as the plane bucked and rocked violently, hit by ground turbulence. Luckily as the lead plane, we did not hit the airstream of the line of other Hercs behind, which I learned later bounced one like a ping-pong ball. "Who are you?" The JMs yelled at us. "Airborne! All the way!" Then it was like I was in a surreal dream as the adrenaline surged. "One minute...GO!!" The number 1 ahead of me was a MG gunner, had thrown his static line, then launched himself out the door, with a helping push by Sergeant Rock. I shuffled to the door, threw my static line forward, then eying the grinning Rockheim pivoted 90 degrees, gripping my belly reserve hurtled out the door!

After a few turbulent, lightning fast seconds, I first recall the chute opening. Jerked back to reality, I felt the adrenaline surging as the Herc roared off disgorging its forty odd paras. The first thing out though was the ramp load, containing our platoon's heavy gear the toboggans. I gripped the risers as I descended, looking up as the next Herc roared overhead. "Whew! Airborne!" I yelled, trying to make out the DZ below, the dozens of chutes descending around me. It was a moonlit night, so I saw the frozen lake below, with the shadows of our chutes outlined by the moonlight. It was sometime around 02:00 A.M. and we had jumped around 800 feet, so it was a short journey to Earth. Around 500 feet, I released the waist band, grabbed my shoulder load (C2 rifle strapped to my snowshoes) then looking below saw the way was clear. No other jumpers close by. Below 200 feet now, I flicked the two quick releases, dropping my rucksack and shoulder load. I kicked the rig cord to get the load swaying, then got ready for the landing. I took a last look around, seeing the blinking lights on the lake. Different colors indicated our Commando RV points, ours was blue I think. "Relax, feet knees together. Tuck chin in. Roll" I recalled the training at Greisbach Training Center, then I hit the ice. It went to plan and I lay gasping in the snow, checking myself and then my gear. Struggling up I looked around, seeing a few dark figures nearby. It was quiet, apart from the noise of the overhead Hercs.

I retrieved my ruck and shoulder load, packed my chute into the attached retainer bag and marched off to the blinking green light.[4] Minutes later, I stood in the RV. point with a dozen soldiers, watching as the remaining chutes came down. It was not long before we knew something was wrong. "There should be allot more chutes than that!" One guy muttered, I did not know who. We were told at the RV only our aircraft had been given the green light.

"OK guys, go bring in our toboggans. Gilligan? You will report to the Ground crew. Bring all your kit and do whatever they tell you. Understand?" I nodded to the Sarge, picked up my gear and trudged through the snow to where the DZ ground crew were in the center of Round Lake. "Trooper Gilligan, 10 Platoon. Here to assist." I reported to Sergeant Collins, who was the Regimental DZ controller and manifest guy. "Good Gill, help the Pathfinders unload their snowmobiles, then you will post sentry on the perimeter. Good man. Off you go."

Scotty was an iconic paratrooper, who had served with the Regiment almost since its conception in 1967. Unflappable, cool headed, I never saw anything unhinge him. Seeing him decades later at the 2018 Airborne

---

4   Each Commando (4 platoons) RV was ID'd by a red, green or blue light at night when most tactical jumps occur

Reunion, he looked almost the same. White hair, grizzled face and smiling. After getting the snowmobiles running, I jumped on one and given a lift to my sentry position, some distance off on the shoreline. The Pathfinder dude, told me to keep alert, for this was a fully tactical winter exercise. "There may be enemy patrols nearby. Challenge everything and report any suspicious activity. No coping any Z's. Questions?"

I shook my head, the snowmobile roared off and began digging into the snow with my snowshoes. I dug a shallow fox hole, sat on my ruck and positioned the FN automatic rifle. By now it was loaded with a magazine of 30 blank rounds. Sleep? How could one? I chuckled as I surveyed the area, a copse of fir trees. I shuddered, tucking my chin inside the arctic parka and scarf. It was a good start for me, having my first jump with the regiment, and I was healthy! The next day we found out what happened. Only the first Herc had unloaded their jumpers of the 24 in total. The second plane had trouble getting its ramp down, therefore could not drop its paras, so all the following aircraft were "stop dropped." Thus, they had to return to the airhead at Trenton. After unfreezing the hydraulics, the ramps worked. Then they loaded up and returned to Round Lake. But in that eerily quiet woods in the middle of a bitterly cold January night, other thoughts were on my mind.

I rechecked my C2 rifle, the bipod extended, rested on the edge of my hole. I cocked the action, cleared the breech and checked the loaded magazine was not clogged with snow. Then replacing it, I cocked the action and put a round up the spout. I flicked the action from Safe (S), to repetition (R) to Automatic (A) then back to safe. The excitement and adrenaline had vanished by now, replaced by icy biting northern winds, sending shivers down my spine. I reminded myself I was no rookie at this, spending several years in infantry units, much of it in dung holes like Round Lake. I spent the rest of that night guarding my section of the perimeter of DZ Chevrolet. I stretched and moved periodically to keep alert and avoiding frostbite. My mind went over a myriad of thoughts, as first light slowly approached. Finally I tensed, hearing faint noise of footsteps at my 12 o'clock. Before my barrel two figures slowly materialized from the dark gloom. As they neared, I saw they were wearing the winter white outer layer and white cammed helmet, snowshoes and carrying 9 mm SMG's.

I flicked the change lever to R and challenged them. "Halt...advance one and be recognized," I hissed. They were about 10 meters to my front by now. Slowly the lead guy approached directly in front of me. "Halt. Pegasus," I whispered. I heard 'Strike', the second part of the Regimental password. Seconds later the two-man patrol squatted at my side. I relaxed, flicked the safety on and listened as they talked. It turned out the patrol were Corporal McClean and Trooper Lebeau of the Pathfinders, who they said had jumped in several days before.

"So yer Gilligan." Lebeau cried with a sly grin. "How did the first jump go?"

"Fuck all" I deadpanned grinning back. Corporal McClean looked me in the eyes. "were you scared?" "Hey, I'm here aren't I?" After a brief chat, they shouldered their rucks and made for the regimental RV out on the ice. McClean's parting words were keep a sharp eye out, the Regiment would jump at first light. I checked the luminous dial of my watch...03:30 AM. About three hours later, I was relieved by another trooper, at last. I beetled my butt to the Commando RV. As I trudged over the ice in my snowshoes, the light was just starting to add definition to the desolate surroundings. Finally, I saw the green light and jogged toward it.

"Hey Gill! Over here buddy, got any smokes?" Trooper Higgins greeted me after arriving. I reported my sit-rep to the Platoon Sergeant, then had a smoke with Higgy. Shortly afterward, a weird apparition greeted my squinting eyes. It looked like a giant UFO I joked, as it loomed up out of the slowly brightening skyline. The blinking lights grew in size, we could now make out the drone of engines. "The Regiment has arrived!" This from Trooper LeClair, another 10 Platoon soldier. "About fucking time! I'm half frozen on this damned lake!" Higgins responded.

It was first light, I watched excited as the blinking lights off in the distance signalled the flight of Hercs approaching. "Here they come guys!" Standing and stomping our stiff feet, our small group watched in fascination as the approaching Hercules transports headed straight at us. It was a fantastic sight, awe inspiring even, one I will never forget. We watched as a WDI was tossed from the lead aircraft's open side door. Scotty would be measuring wind speed and direction, relaying the data to the lead C-130. Then the first bodies started disgorging from the lead Herc. This time the ramps worked as well, the pallets slid off and dangled below large cargo chutes to perfection. Soon the air above was filled with long streams of green and white parachutes. Muffled shouts reached us from high above, as hundreds of paratroopers descended, jostling in a mass to land safely on the frozen lake.

"Keep your head up Gill buddy." A trooper warned me, as this was my first mass parachute drop. With so many chutes in the air, it was a potentially hazardous place to be at that moment, so do not get overwhelmed by the sights and sounds. As the first six C-130's finished dropping their loads, they banked off and headed back for Trenton. Then the next group of planes roared overhead. Again figures appeared out the side doors, then we heard the crack as the chutes opened. I was reminded of 82nd Airborne's slogan, "Death from above" as paras thudded down all over the lake. I watched as the last four planes emptied their fuselages of their jumpers. Then our blood froze, as we heard the screams from above. Scanning the sky, I saw two paras in trouble. Their main chutes were entangled, one a streamer, the other a partial malfunction. "Holy shit!" I thought, watching the two bodies descend rapidly toward the lake. They hit about 100 meters off, bouncing off the ice with a sickening thud. I was stunned, mesmerized by the scene, two of my brothers lying in a pile with their gear.

I was sure they must have perished, later learning that miraculously they had survived. They were from 1 Commando, French from Quebec most likely. Both had been badly injured, broken legs, pelvis and such, probably never to jump again. Soon after they were medivacked out, loaded onto sleds and pulled by snowmobiles to waiting ambulances. As well it turned out, they were not alone. Well over 100 from the Airborne that jumped that morning were injured. Including my 3 Commando OC Major Leavy who we heard had cracked an ankle. Meanwhile the survivors beetled over the lake, collecting our toboggans, assisting in unloading snowmobiles, jeeps and 1 ton trucks from the big pallet loads. It was late morning by the time we were organized into our platoons for the upcoming march.

We heard there had been casualties, but the number kept rising to over 200. They called it "The Round Lake Massacre," later many of us purchased Airborne t-shirts with the motto displayed. This was after we returned to base after End-Ex. The Bear, Major Leavy tried to gut it out on his broken ankle, but soon had to be medivacked out. For me during the march, I spent much of that day in the traces, pulling the toboggan. We marched all day, trudging through snow, leaving Round Lake behind, never to be seen again. It was a long hump, even though it was cold, I started sweating. We had nothing to drink, as our canteens were frozen solid, so I munched on snow by the trail in the deep snow. I started to hallucinate, like a dying man crossing a desert.

We camped later that night, erected our tents and brewed up. My NCO Miles passed out the sentry list, briefing us on the SitRep from Commando HQ. Most of us ate then passed out cigarettes as we lay on our air mattresses, enjoying the break. I chatted with the boys, joking about my wager with the Sarge. "Well PB I'm still here." McClean replied we were just getting started, with about two weeks in the sticks to go. It was a series of marches, till we bumped into the enemy force one night. We were trying to find these militia, who were acting as the enemy. It was dark out as 3 Commando marched along a hill. I looked down into a valley, my eyes seeing the dim shape of tents below. I alerted the platoon and we halted. After confirming it was our illusive foe, we did a quick assault. We surprised the enemy in their tents and bagged a platoon. Just another day in the 'Borne.

We marched on, reaching our final objective days later. Bonnechere Airport. We attacked with all three companies and seized the airstrip and surrounding buildings. It was the Airborne's major coup, capturing and holding this vital objective. To commemorate it, HQ & Signals Squadron jumped in, including the Regiment CO Colonel Bucky Douglas. I watched from my OP in a nearby copse of woods, as the chutes descended to land near the airport's plowed runways. Bucky did not have to walk far to his waiting jeep.

"Well Bucky decided to join us eh?" One of my platoon mates yelled joyously. It was now into our third week in the bush, so we needed humour. We laughed at the thinly veiled satire of our beloved CO. The best part was we knew, if Bucky was here, it was near End Ex. To confirm our suspicions, about an hour later the glorious words greeted our frozen ears.

"End Ex! Alright 10 Platoon on me!" Trooper Thomas yelled over, "Hell yeah! There goes PB. Let's go Gill!" As we gathered our rucks and headed to the road, we heard the welcoming roar of 5 and 2 ½ ton trucks roaring down the road. We climbed aboard our land taxis, arriving back at CFB Petawawa later that afternoon. I had survived my first Regimental Winter Exercise, collecting my bet in beer from PB later. There would be many more to follow, the next one a few weeks later at Earlton, further north in Northern Ontario.

At the time, in the Canadian Armed Forces the SSF to which the Airborne were attached, was one of the mostly competent, highly trained combat units in the Western world. Our reason detre was to protect Canada's North, in sub-arctic and arctic conditions. We had learned survival, now it was pushed to a new level, excelling in a hostile, imposing environment. For individual soldiers like me, I strove to be a well honed, motivated team member. We could afford no weak links, which could spell disaster for all. Thus many ended their careers early in the 'Borne. As winter training continued, I gradually ticked off the myriad of objectives to complete the list in my pay level. I was also receiving jump pay now as a paratrooper.

After a weekend off to recover, the Commando geared up for the next big winter exercise. For the next few weeks, it was normal garrison routine. Morning runs, weapons cleaning, gear inspections and paperwork. Everything was good as I prepared for my next big airborne ex. The regiment jumped onto DZ Frost, at Earlton on February 8. I was slotted in at #9 Port side that night. It was called Ex. Lightning Strike, my second tactical night jump with the regiment. We were loaded down with heavier loads, staggering in the bucking, heaving plane as we prayed for the light to turn green. Then I saw the ramp load leave, the green came on and we launched forward out the door. As I approached the door, I felt excited but mentally aware of my surroundings, the noise, vibrations of the C-130 airframe, each jumper doing his job. We were like a machine as rapidly the sticks shuffled forward, disgorging a para every few seconds. Then I was there, standing in the door. The strain of the heavy load vanished as I launched out the door. The blast of wintry air hit me, taking my breath away as I was whipped away in the prop blast. After four seconds the main cracked open, jerking on my rig harness. I have had bruises on my groin and shoulders from these hard openings. Some 'Borne jumpers had their helmets ripped off, riser burns on their neck and faces. As I learned over the coming years, this was not a job for anyone. Hence the demanding training courses and physical endurance required. As I touched down on the DZ Frost, I knew I had 9 jumps, yet I was still on the long journey to becoming a trained paratrooper. For this mass drop, things went well, with few casualties, the Regiment had learned its lessons apparently from Round Lake.

Then the real work began. A few minutes of adrenaline rushed excitement, followed by long days of regular infantry work. We marched with all our gear across country on some compass heading into the arctic abyss. I can only guess how far we humped that first day or the next. We as riflemen in the companies followed orders. It was get your gear on and march, one snowshoe step at a time, hour after hour. Periodically every couple of hours or so, we halted for short breaks. The men at the point consulted maps, radioed SitRep in to Regimental HQ, letting them know where our 3 Commando was on the tactical map. Each Commando company marched along separate routes to cover a larger territory and probably ease congestion.

A practical example of this was the famous Battle of Arnhem in WW2. As part of Operation Market Garden, the biggest Airborne drop in history, three full Airborne divisions (40,000 men) landed in Holland behind German lines to seize key roads and bridges. The British 1st Airborne Division with the attached Polish Brigade, somewhere around 20,000 paras jumped or landed by glider in Northern Holland tasked with seizing the key Arnhem Bridges. If successful, the next stop would be Berlin and the end of the war in Europe. The DZ was not at the bridge but over 12 miles away. To seize the bridge, the division advanced in separate battalions using different routes. Much as we did that exercise, 2 Para (2nd Battalion, The Parachute Regiment) arrived at the northern end of the main bridge in Arnhem and seized it in a quick lightning attack. Colonel Frost the CO, immortalized in the movie *A Bridge to Far*, attempted to seize the southern end by dashing a company across the long span. It was a failure and was repulsed with heavy losses. The valiant British Paras were surrounded by two full SS Panzer divisions, their luck slowly running out. Relief columns all failed to get to 2 Para over that week. Finally, out of ammunition and food, most of the wounded survivors of 2 Para surrendered to the Germans. In 1985 while on holidays from my UN Duty in Cyprus, I visited the Airborne cemeteries in Holland. For a young paratrooper like I was, it was a sober eye opener. As I walked along the long lines of crosses the full brunt of war hit me like a fist.

After the day's march, we bivouacked for the evening. It was becoming routine by now. Each section was timed by the NCO in charge. Our tents had to be up, erect with lantern and stove lit, in like under ten minutes. The officers gathered for their O-group (orders re-org) as we brewed up and had our first meal that day. Most of us were smokers by now, lighting up as we lay exhausted on our air mattresses, after unpacking our rucks in the tent. One guy tended the stove and lantern, then sentries were posted on the perimeter, the Section I/C arrived and gave us the SitRep for the night and the next day. We had come approximately 12 km.'s, maybe a quarter of the way to our main objective. This was the northern Ontario town of Earlton. We would be approaching in three prongs, surround the town and capture the airstrip. Then like Round Lake, our CO, Colonel Bucky would arrive triumphantly, jumping on the captured airstrip with Regimental HQ. We listened quietly, eyeing one another as the information came at us. Some grimaced, some smiled, raising an eyebrow, blowing rings of smoke in the air. But no one bitched or protested, we buckled down and got 'er done in Airborne fashion. Over the next week, we steadily approached the objective, getting bumped by the enemy all the way. We took out these obstacles by small unit actions, which built gradually toward the end in a full on regimental or battalion assault. Our CQ (Quartermaster Stores) followed us in trucks, resupplying us with rations and ammo as we depleted our personal load.

After ten days or so, we reached Earlton...finally. It was the first sign of civilization I had seen in days. Humans could be seen living there, whereas all I had seen for days were snow and trees. As I said before, on field ex., we soldiers slowly transformed into virtual animals. With a lack of water, we did not wash or shave. We started growing beards, our dirty, stained clothing took on the shade of our environment...natural camouflage. No need for expensive, pretty camouflage clothing back then. We were filthy, faces stained with dirt, blackened by fumes, smoke and cordite from the thousands of rounds fired. Like everyone else who made it, I metamorphed into a new life form, ready for anything the nasty world could throw at me. We even had a term for it, hitting the wall and pushing past it. Every person has a limit, where you leave it "all out there." In the airborne each Para was taught how to get there, then push past. It was part physical to get there, but all mental to push on. You learned to set new limits, goals to spur yourself on, when mentally you were done in!

The final assault when it came, was as a sort of euphoric rush to us. One saw the full power of the Regiment on display for the first time. Every weapon in our arsenal unleashed on our enemy, surrounded and pinned to their defensive position. Unfortunately, we used dummy ammo. Otherwise the town of Earlton would have been flattened by our pent up and now unleashed rage. Still it was impressive, as clouds of smoke drifted in the air, explosions echoed from pyrotechnic "dummy artillery," the crackle of machine guns and small arms growing in intensity, like a symphonic orchestra building to a climax. As each company engaged, the racket grew, even E Battery and Recon Squadron of the 8th CH, our airborne armour support joined in. Finally, my platoon joined the assault, advancing on the defensive position in 2-3 man groups.

I formed part of the cover fire with my automatic rifle as the final riflemen went past and secured the enemy objective, took prisoners and bayoneted anything that moved. Finally flares arced into the sky and whistles blew. The assault was over! That night we bivouacked in our tents in high spirits. Bucky was expected soon, then End-Ex and back to the world! As it turned out, it was not the end of the exercise. We spent a week in a company defensive position, building snow defenses, regular night patrols and maintaining strict tactical alertness.

The CO did reward us finally, by giving the order to issue our field rum ration. I have heard this was inherited from the Royal Navy, where every sailor received a daily rum ration at sea. The British Army adopted it later, then passed on the tradition to our Canadian Army. It was voluntary and deducted from your pay, so you could decline it. I did not, nor most of my platoon mates. There was not enough to get drunk on, it was maybe a cup full, but some of our attached militia who did not drink, declined it. For me personally, I embraced this tradition, as part of being a trained soldier. In no way, did it impede my performance or demands laid on me. Which leads to the next part of my tale. Finally after a week spent in our defensive positions around the town, early that morning, we heard a surprise 'bug-out' being called. It was panic time, as we had about 10 minutes to pack everything up and be on the road ready to march. I remember it was a flurry of rushing bodies, packing our rucks, tearing the tent down, packing gear into the sled and racing to the nearby road. Ten minutes later, we had done it,3 Commando stood in ranks on the road before Major Leavy and the HQ officers. Then we saw a problem, back at our bivouac site, one solitary tent still remained! Major Leavy saw it too, all seeing the grim displeasure on his face, as he glared in anger. "Whose tent is that? Lieutenant go find out!" Seconds later we watched as the harassed officer stuck his face into the tent. Seconds later the perpetrator emerged, none other than our platoon sergeant McClean. He had obviously been asleep, as we stared he emerged, struggling into his uniform. Our platoon struggled to remain silent, as the Senior NCO reported to the Major. It was ugly, even pathetic, as the disgraced NCO was ordered to get on a vehicle back to base. It turned out later, he had thieved a good part of our platoon's rum ration for himself, getting drunk for the past few days.

For us End Ex was called shortly afterward. We marched a short distance to the waiting convoy of trucks, then the long ride back to CFB Petawawa. Later that day, Colonel Douglas debriefed us at the base gym, after we had cleaned weapons and turned in our toboggans and other borrowed gear. The CO praised us for a job well done, accomplishing our goals during the Ex. We nodded, shouting Airborne as we stood in massed ranks in the gym. I was impressed by the high morale, the esprit-de-corps, displayed by over 800 paratroopers inside the building. Later Major Leavy addressed 3 Commando. "Men, we work hard. But we also party hard! Good job, our winter training is over till next year. We have courses coming up, so you have the weekend off. Enjoy it, be back early on Monday morning, we will go for a little run to stretch our legs. Airborne! Dismiss the Commando NCO's!" Our platoon responded vigorously, responding Airborne, then we had two days off to celebrate. I did not see our ex Platoon Sergeant, till years later. He was kicked out of the Regiment in disgrace, RTU'd back to his former regiment the RCR. The lesson to all of us was, never let your guard down.

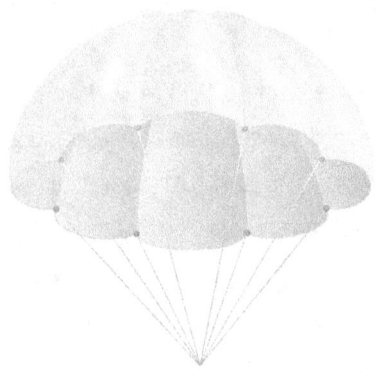

Continuation Training

By April 1984, I had completed the Winter Warfare qualification, including a Battle School. This included a live grenade assault at a range bunker, platoon defensive position, building snow defenses, section attack, Nordic skiing, AFV recognition and anti-tank methods. One way to destroy an armoured vehicle is to fix a sticky bomb or mine to the track or hull. We dug a foxhole and camouflaged it, let the armoured vehicle roll by, then spring out and climb aboard to fix the mine, then run for it. This was the most hazardous, a last-ditch measure when our defensive position is being overrun by superior forces. But it had stopped a major German counter-attack in Normandy after D-Day. It had been used frequently on the Russian front by both sides, as there were large numbers of tanks involved in most assaults. Canadian infantry were also equipped with several anti-tank weapons, including the M-72 (one shot disposable rocket launcher) and the 84mm Karl Gustav rocket launcher. Also, every infantry battalion had an intrinsic Heavy weapons company, armed with TOW wire guided rocket launchers. Artillery units had M-109 tracked vehicles armed with 155 mm howitzers. The Airborne Regiment had E Battery, part of The Airborne Battle Group, armed with four air deployable 105 mm guns.

The typical anti-tank team were two men, attached to the company heavy weapons platoon. In 3 Commando, this HW platoon also included 81 mm mortars, our indirect fire support. The Regimental Battle Group was also supported by E Battery Para, part of 2 RCHA, armed with four 105mm howitzers, which could be air dropped. I was also trained on the 60-mm light mortar, issued to each platoon. Even though I rarely carried it, I usually packed several mortar bombs in my rucksack, along with a week supply of bullets for my personal weapons.

Most of this was merely a refresher training for I had previously taken it, before being attached to 3 Commando. For some reason, HQ did not acknowledge it, which was up to the Commanding Officer, Major Leavy. However, by June I was finished with the basic infantry qualifications. One new thing added, was an Escape& Evasion exercise, in March of that year. This exercise is used by Special Forces worldwide, to train operatives when behind enemy lines to avoid capture. Also, it is designed to assess individuals if captured, to handle rough treatment and interrogation, including torture methods. Conducted at the platoon level, we were issued with winter survival gear as it was still winter.

We had a week issue of rations, a packet of matches, but no weapons, stoves or tents. We were dropped off by truck in Algonquin Park, north of Petawawa, in teams of three. From there we had a week to cross the huge park to a safe area. We were told the rules were no breaking of civilian laws, anyone we saw was the enemy, including the OPP. It was sprang on us as a surprise, following the end of the Winter field exercises. As we stood on the road that cold March day, we looked at each other stunned. One trooper, Shirley I believe had a map and compass, so after getting orientated, we set off down the road. We were not amused by the rough treatment dished out to us. Initially we had been jumped, a sack over our heads and tied up. Any movement or sound as we lay on the floor, resulted in the enemy pouring water over the sack, which caused us to struggle to breathe. It was scary being blind and helpless, the enemy taunting us and kicking our legs. But the water boarding was the worst, the closest I came to panicking in my life. As we clumped down the road, we talked over the situation, eventually arriving at a plan. An hour or so later, we reached the first checkpoint on our route. As instructed we wrote out names on a paper, then sat down for a quick meal. Shortly after a second group met up with us. Then we decided on what to do next. It was an unconventional approach to Escape & Evasion. We set up a makeshift roadblock, pulling a few dead trees onto the road. Then we waited for vehicles to run into it. After shivering and stomping in the snow for a while, we heard the roar of an engine.

"OK guys, here it comes! We stop it and say we are on Exercise and desperately need a lift. Our vehicle broke down and our radio battery is dead." So we waited on the side of that desolate road on that cold, bleary day, as the vehicle, a mobile camper slowed to a stop. The ruse worked, as the elderly retired couple were happy to assist us. Overjoyed we climbed aboard, the old gentlemen smiling at us, then he calmly drove the camper down the road. We added a small detail as we reached the second checkpoint in minutes.

One soldier, Larry LeClair raced to the board to write down our names, by then six of us. We told the driver that should he be stopped down the road, to say that he had not seen us. We explained this was an exercise, our cruel enemy was forcing us to survive in the cold wilderness, at the mercy of the elements, freezing and starving. The old lady gasped in shock upon hearing this, offering us a thermos of hot coffee. We grinned at her, taking the thermos from her hand, then fighting for the first gulp of delicious brew! It turned out to be a glorious success, as that afternoon, we rapidly advanced through the park, checking off over a dozen check points. On foot, it would have taken us the balance of that week. In fact, as we found out later, our group was the only one not to be captured. Most did not make it very far, spending the remainder of the week in a police jail cell. As we neared the finish line, we got increasingly nervous, expecting the enemy (our platoon officer and NCO's) to stop us at a checkpoint soon.

So, we advised the old driver to deny seeing us if asked. We reinforced to the old couple the lack of sympathy these guys had for us. They bought in hook line and sinker, for soon afterward were stopped at a checkpoint. As we hid in the back, the dear old couple played the ignorance game. Like the Greeks in the Trojan horse, we sniggered as the old guy was waved through by the unsuspecting 'Trojan guard!' As we laughed our way to the next checkpoint and finish line, we then argued over what to do next. For as we knew, the exercise was to last for about 10 days. The Lieutenant had figured it would take us at least that long to walk over 150 kilometers in the dead of winter. We had completed it in about four hours. Should we turn ourselves in? Would they then lock us up in the jail out of spite?

In the end, we decided not to chance it. The old couple let us off in the nearest town of Whitby, on the edge of the park, bidding us luck. It was over 200 km. back to CFB Petawawa and it was getting dark. Needing a place of refuge, someone suggested the local church. We knocked on the church door, then the RC priest listened to our tale with a look of pity. He welcomed us inside, our first warm building since leaving the base that morning. In the end the priest fed us and issued us a pack of cigarettes. The next day after a nice snooze, we set off, smoking cigarettes and telling crude jokes. Now we decided to push for the base at full speed, aware that the enemy might be lurking around the next corner. Hitting the main highway, we hitchhiked south that morning. Again, we had luck, arriving back at the base gates in the early afternoon. We dutifully reported to the duty NCO and left our names, informing him we were on a field exercise. He stared at our forlorn appearances, but waved us through. As tired as we were, we raced for our barracks, laughing most of the way. We got the barracks NCO to let us in our rooms, then stripping off our dirty clothes raced for the showers. It was sheer luxury, I never appreciated a simple shower as much as then, since we were resigned to go without for at least a full week! Later dressed in clean civilian clothes, we had a nice meal in the mess, then headed for the drinking mess. So as our platoon mates eked it out in the cold of Algonquin Park, or sat in dank cells, the six of us partied with the local women and got gloriously drunk!

It was SOP for soldiers, to follow up a mission success with copious amounts of alcohol and young ladies! Just ask the recently famous US Navy Seals, who like us, would not lose a minute of sleep in twisting the rules in order to achieve success. One only has a set time on Earth, so our attitude is to enjoy your time, wherever and whenever possible. Of course, this attitude is frowned upon, as I was to be reminded of in the not to distant future.

But that week, we took full advantage of our freedom and glory of being Airborne paratroopers! As the week ended, we awoke each morning, joking about what the platoon were doing. No morning PT, we sauntered over to the mess for steaming hot coffee, bacon and eggs. Then stretching our legs a bit, hit the base store to buy cigarettes and other luxury items. We caught up on our sleep during the day, stuffed ourselves at meal times, then hit the bars again at night. Finally, the world caught up to us eventually as that blissful week came to an end.

    Our beloved Platoon Commander, Captain Beaudoin who was in a state of frustration at his failure to find the missing six, called into base. I have heard some thought we had perished in the wilderness, a full out search and rescue with choppers and all being called in. The officer called the base in a near panic, before calmly being told that we were in fact, safe and sound, arriving at the base five days ago. He was nearly apoplectic as he heard the surprise news! Then he ordered the MP's to round us up and throw us in the base jail cells. As we arrived some time later, most of us still hung over, we exchanged stories on our night in town and where the hated screws (MP's) had caught us. After the End Ex was called a few days later, the platoon arrived back at base. We were pulled out of the MP shack, subsequently charged and marched in front of 'the Bear', Major Leavy. Captain Beaudoin had charged us with refusing to obey a lawful order, the catch phrase for mostly anything. It could mean jail or a fine, as we stood before a grim-faced C.O. of 3 Commando. After listening to our explanation, particularly the platoon OC's orders, not mentioning that we should not hitch hike, the Major dismissed all the charges. In fact, he commended us on using our personal initiative, while in a very stressful situation. "Good job men. That is the type of soldier I want in my outfit! Dismissed, oh Captain, I will have a word with you if you please!" I believe he was reprimanded, blaming his soldiers for his own failure as the exercise commander. Luckily for us, he never got another chance at us, to repeat the Escape & Evasion. It did teach me one important lesson though, never surrender, never give in under any situation. It is one of those life lessons, remaining with me for decades.

After the successful conclusion of the Escape & Evasion Ex., the spring of 1984 rolled on. 3 Commando did a continuation drop on DZ Anzio, Petawawa on 23rd March. It was my first on this drop zone, one of many to come. In a three-plane formation of C-130 Hercules, I was #19 Port side, on this administrative jump wearing full equipment. It was a rare daylight drop but was called off due to bad weather. We tried again a week later March 30. This was a go, this time I was slotted in at #18 Starboard side. It was exciting for me, my first on Anzio DZ, named after the famous battle in Italy in 1944. As we approached jump altitude, we went through the standard equipment checks. I stood near the rear of the stick, my senses vibrated as the adrenaline kicked in. Morale was good as we waited patiently, shouting Airborne as the JM's barked out the standard 'Who are you?" The side doors opened, the Crew chief and JM's performing the routine checks. The stand-by order came, the stick leader stood in the door as the red light came on. "Huh-Ya! 3 Commando!" We yelled in a chorus, as the green light came on. The sticks started moving before me, I held the static line in my left hand as I shuffled forward as the jumpers ahead exited in quick succession. Then my turn...I threw the static line forward to the JM, pivoted in the door and looked out at the DZ 1000 feet below.

I gripped my rucksack, tucked my chin down and sprang forward. It was my tenth jump, so I clearly recall how it unfolded. I was whipped sideways by the roaring prop blast, the noise deafening, then saw the para ahead of me, his CT-1 round chuted cracking open below. A few seconds later my chute opened with a crack, jerking me in the harness. The noise dissipated rapidly as the C-130 roared off, my eyes staring at the last few jumpers exiting. I was ecstatic, my first glimpse of this as I floated down to the DZ. I was in the midst of over 100 chutes, stretched out in a long line over the drop zone. Then it was back to business, checking around me for other jumpers. The drills took over as I dropped, releasing the waistband, dropping my shoulder load with weapon, then below 200 feet, flicked the quick releases, dropping my gear. Seeing the ground rush up, I assumed the landing position, hit and rolled. I whooped in joy as I stood up, seeing other paras all around me. I unhooked and slipped out of the harness, stretching in the suns rays, thanking the gods I was alive! Some jumpers lit up cigarettes, others relieved themselves in the DZ grass. Then packing up our gear, trotted over to the platoon RV point, dropping the chutes off. Then 3 Commando formed up on the dirt road for the march back to the base about 10 kilometers away.

I was part of four more jumps on DZ Anzio that spring, two in April and two in May. April 4 was a tactical equipment jump with rifle and webbing. I was #3 Starboard side in the C-130 this time, another daylight jump. It was part of a tactical exercise, where 3 Commando would assault the Arnprior dam. The mass drop went to plan, then we quickly reorganized into our platoons after dropping off our chutes at the RV's. CH-147 Chinook helicopters landed for the flight to Arnprior. We ran up the rear ramp door, cramming into the big dual rotor medium lift choppers. I came to love this chopper, in my view the best heavy chopper in the world, still in use 30 years later, an indispensable part of Special Forces Ops in the Middle East and around the planet. We sat in comfortable folding seats for the hour-long flight. The rear ramp was partially lowered to give us an excellent view of the surrounding countryside. Finally, we landed in a field, a few fields away from the dam. My section split off, led by my section commander, M/Cpl Donny Gallagher. He gave us a quick O-group, then we rushed across the field toward the dam. It was a lightning assault, capturing the dam in minutes. Then we boarded the Chinooks again for the trip back to base. I was satisfied with my performance to date, things were going smoothly as I approached my first-year anniversary, so to speak. On April 19, my 12th jump was out of the Chinook, for the first time. It was also my first ramp jump, as the Chinook has no side doors. I was #9 Port side, as we stood in two rows of about ten jumpers, staring ahead as the ramp lowered, giving us a perfect view of the DZ below. It was new to me, as we exited off the ramp, we threw the static line, then simply ran off and sprang into the breeze. It was easy I thought, no prop blast, less noise and frenzied exit into a whirlwind! I recall you could feel yourself falling as the ground rose slowly below. Then the chute cracked above, amidst the line of dangling paras. "I'm getting a hard on!" I yelled over the nearest jumper, who whooped and shouted Airborne.

The landing was not so ideal, as I was blown backward while descending. After lowering my load, I looked over my shoulder, seeing I was headed for an old bomb crater. I knew this DZ was formerly a live range, so was potted with craters made by shells long ago. It was something I had trained for in Jump school, a rear landing, left or right. My ruck hit then me, landing on the tip of the crater, then rolling backwards like a ball down the crater. I finished up at the bottom, tangled in the chute and lines. I had to be assisted out of the crater, complaining of a sore neck. I caught a ride to the base MIR, where they examined me and took some x-rays. The Doc told me I had a compressed disc in my neck, luckily nothing was broken. I nodded thankfully, asking how long this would last. He replied probably a lifetime, possibly getting worse as I got older. I was 26 and in my prime at this time, so I brushed it off.

As it turned out I was right. I felt twinges in my neck for the next year or so, especially when doing route marches with heavy loads. Eventually it slowly went away, to leave me to continue my duties in the 'Borne. Returned to full duties a few days later, we continued our routine PT and other duties, shooting on the ranges and such. During the nights off, I accompanied other platoon mates to celebrate in the base drinking messes, as well as Pembroke and Ottawa as time allowed. My focus now was on completing my first year, doing the Airborne Indoctrination Course (hell week) and finally...receive my Airborne coin. Don Gallagher my direct superior, told me I would do this in August to September coming up. In May, I did two more jumps, both standard administrative day-equipment drops on DZ Anzio. These both went perfect, so my confidence returned, it was full speed ahead. On May 29, 3 Commando were to parachute, on Dives Crossing, part of Mattawa Plain, next to the Ottawa River. It was stop-dropped at the last minute due to high winds. It was here in 1968, that the worst drop in Canadian Airborne history occurred. On May 8, 26 paras jumped from three Buffalo aircraft on the Mattawa Plain. Rough winds blew them east into the frigid Ottawa River. Seven drowned before rescue boats got to them. [5]

The main force of the SSF Brigade landed on the Mattawa Plain in Chinook dual rotor choppers, as well as Huey single rotor choppers. It was a tactical exercise, so we carried a full load, rations, several hundred rounds and assorted equipment. My section was clearing the surrounding woods for enemy, when I showed my keen eyesight. I was alone as I probed the thick foliage, then entered a small clearing. I looked around, then my spider senses started tingling. I knew something was funny, so stopped as our section pushed rapidly through the woods. Then I saw it, a radio antennae sticking out of a nearby clump of brush and grass.

"Hey Corporal! Come look at this!" M/Cpl Miles my 10 Platoon section commander arrived, then I walked to the antennae. As I reached for it, my foot collapsed the camouflaged shelter which was practically invisible. Miles smiled as he ripped it way, the two enemy crouching down in the cleverly concealed slit trench. The two captured enemy got out, saying they were from 1 RCR, congratulating me on finding them. "No big deal guys. It's what I do. Airborne!" After turning over the prisoners to the Platoon HQ, we pressed on. It was a standard advance to contact, the entire Airborne Regiment an integral part of the SSF Brigade. This was Canada's

---

5 "Into the Icy Waters" Pg. 48-52; LEGION MAG. May/June 2018.

quick reaction force, our Special Forces of the day. Over the next few days we advanced rapidly, attacking in progressively larger formations up to Brigade final attack. It was termed Exercise Final Fling, our last tactical Ex before the summer. After End Ex was called, we trooped wearily out to the waiting trucks. Most of us had little or no sleep for the three-day ex. I was tired but elated at the end, having personally gone near a week with sleep deprivation.

We road the trucks back to base, some of the platoons force marching back in Airborne fashion. Back at base, we relaxed, smoking cigarettes and taking some water for the first time in ages. We were tired, filthy from digging holes but in high morale. For as the weekend was approaching, the CO rewarded us for a job well done with a few days off. After we stripped and cleaned weapons, using varsol baths to remove dirt, rust and carbon fouling, we went over every part, meticulously cleaning the bore, trigger mechanism, then reassembled, we turned them in at the Stores compound. After our platoon was addressed by the platoon commander Captain Beaudoin, dismissed we raced for the barracks like children let out of school… more or less! After a quick shower, we ate at the mess then hit the bars. As the Bear (Major Leavy) was proud to claim, "We work hard lads! But we also party hard! Airborne!" So, that weekend we did, terrorizing every bar from Petawawa to Toronto to Ottawa. We called this the Maroon Triangle. In July, I had completed my first year in 3 Commando, but my Selection phase was not quite over. After annual leave (2 weeks) in July it was back to the grind, daily runs, marches working up to the August push. For me that was Mountain school, three weeks climbing real cliffs in Quebec's Appalachian Mountains, across the Ottawa River. This taught the Airborne paratrooper recruits the basics of mountain warfare, including a large-scale climb and assault on an enemy position on top of the cliff. Then in the final exercise, we used ropes to evacuate our wounded to the ground hundreds of feet below, repelling down rapidly, carrying heavy weapons loads. I learned that for one to succeed it required extreme levels of fitness, stamina and a steely resolve. One of our men, an NCO broke his arm falling onto a cliff precipice. As we loaded him on a stretcher for medivac, we were dangling by fixed ropes. He handed me his small camera, asking me to take a picture to show his wife and kids. As I reluctantly agreed, he smiled and gave the thumbs up as I snapped the pic of him lying strapped onto the stretcher. On the ground we marched back to base camp. The course staff debriefed us, concluding we were now ready to take part in Airborne mountain warfare. Personally, I felt more confident, in excellent physical condition and morale we as good. I would need it as we returned to Petawawa and the Regiment. In August, the final part of Selection, I underwent the Airborne Indoctrination Course (AIC), two weeks of Hell! We awoke at the crack of dawn, formed up for roll call and ran first thing in the morning. It was a gruelling grind, long days and nights, we ran everywhere. No such thing as walking! Most of the time in full battle gear, helmets and weapons. It was blistering hot, the humidity in the northern forests was punishing. Any fat left on the body was burned off, I finished up at around 168 pounds which for me is bare bones!

We did four parachute jumps during the course, the final one a full equipment night jump on DZ Anzio, just north of the base. The final ex was easy, establishing a platoon hide, sending out reconnaissance patrols and perimeter security. Of course, we dug trenches for the next day, camouflaged them and fought off imaginary enemy soldiers. When end ex was called, we loaded up and formed up on the dirt track for the long hump back to base, about 10 kilometers away. Most of us bleary eyed paratroopers were going on adrenaline by now, but we could see the light at the end of the tunnel. We triumphantly reached the main base an hour or so later after the final forced march. Shortly after the course officer addressed us, congratulated us on completing the AIC and presented us with a certificate and the vaunted Airborne coin. It was a surreal moment as he placed it in my hand, the end of 12 months of hard slogging, pain and sacrifice. I was now a fully-fledged Airborne paratrooper.

Beside me that day was one of my old buddies from the Ottawa Cameron Highlanders, Ian Wadleigh. We slapped each other on the back, happy and proud to be wearing maroon berets at last. Dismissed and the AIC done, we reported back to the Commando for duty. The rest of the summer was easy by comparison, a few casual "bare ass" jumps on DZ Anzio as we trained paratroopers from visiting Allied Airborne and Special Forces units. It was enjoyable easy work, designed to acquaint our Allies with Canadian jump procedures and drills. We intermingled with British, American, Australian and NATO Allies during these Jump Bivouacs. Also, hundreds of new paratroopers posted in from Canadian Forces units participated to reacquire Airborne parachuting procedures before we were sent on tactical operations.

Also during that summer, I bought my first vehicle. It was a 1975 Dodge Coronet, which I purchased from Sly Sylvester, one of my mates in 3 Commando. It gave me freedom during days off, in which I travelled from CFB Petawawa up and down the Ottawa Valley. I was spreading my wings so to speak, becoming acquainted with towns like North Bay, Wawa, Pembroke, Arnprior, the village of Petawawa and my home city of Ottawa. My parents lived in the country, 60 kilometers east of the capital near the village of Plantagenet. I drove there to show off my new car, a candy apple red ragtop, the Coronet was my first love. It was an idealic time, an intense feeling of pride and accomplishment in passing every hurdle the Airborne Regiment had thrown up before me. It had by no means been easy, many other inductees had failed to meet the exacting standards and had been sent off to their former units, or released from the Forces all together. Others had been badly injured and could no longer serve as combat soldiers. Some remustered to other trades like the Air Force or Navy.

For myself, I entered the second year of a three-year term with 3 Commando, Airborne Regiment. Having passed Selection, concluded with the AIC Course, I returned to 10 Platoon for ongoing training as an infantry rifleman. In August, the Airborne Regiment having filled the ranks with new replacements, began with FallCon, an annual exercise designed to bring all units up to speed. Beginning on September 17. Fallcon Ex. Lasted until September 28. We marched from the base 10 to 12 kilometers with full gear, weapons and rucksacks. In the deep woods near the Ottawa River, we set up base camp, tents and cooked up rations. It was the usual routine over the next few weeks, beginning with small unit ops, working up to a big combined Regimental Battle Group operation, before concluding the exercise and returning to base at Petawawa. We used Huey transport and Chinook medium lift helicopters frequently to cover huge expanses of rough, heavily forested terrain to assault our enemy force.

Most attacks we used dummy or blank rounds for safety purposes, as many of the new FNG's would probably have resulted in friendly fire. We had to get used to the challenging environment of the northern Ontario forests. Hordes of insects, rain, black bears and of course sleep depravation. Personally, I could handle it, having been an infantry soldier for years. But I have seen some lose it, hallucinating and having a chat with a shrub, rock or tree. Others caught the flu, pneumonia, intestinal infections, stomach poisoning or physical injuries and were medevacked out. My last injury was a cut knee while in West Germany during NATO Flyover Exercises in 1979 and spent a few weeks out of the line recuperating. Fallcon concluded with a three-day tactical exercise from September 25-27, termed Ex. Bear Claw. We operated primarily within our basic platoon of 30 odd soldiers, honing individual and team tasks.

Luckily FallCon went smoothly for my platoon, marching back on to base in high spirits. 10 Platoon was melding together as a team. We were confident, trained to be aggressive in our tasks, taking new replacements under our wing and succeeding in any task handed to us. We were considered an elite regiment, the quick reaction force of the SSF Brigade. Our ongoing training was designed to keep us sharp, ready for deployment to anywhere in Canada or the world at a moments notice. That fall in 1984 we heard of the U.S. attack on Grenada, the first time the U.S. Navy Seals were used in combat since Vietnam. I had little idea of who they were then, being more familiar with the U.S. Marines, 82nd Airborne Division, Green Berets, U.S. Rangers and of course the British Paras and Special Air Service (SAS).

Most of us craved real combat action, for this was supposedly what all the hard-physical training and sacrifices where for. But like any serving soldier, we were at the mercy of our politicians. Many a night in bars, at parties or lying in barracks bunks, we discussed the uncertain future. Would we see war, would we perish or be injured? Or would we be lucky enough to miss action and die old men? As we say, only time and the Gods would tell us the answer. After this intense training, we were rewarded for our hard work by the C.O. We disappeared for the weekend, travelling to faraway places, to forget about the Army and relax and sample the nightlife. Airborne soldiers were young (19-23 years old) so we preyed upon the young women in bars.

The older NCO's and officers were mostly married with families, so they stayed separate, retiring to more sedate home life and more mundane daily activities. I would comment here, it was a sign of the times, in the early 80's, that soldiers were hard drinkers, while some did drugs. Some of the younger soldiers fell afoul of the law, charged for some minor offence, sometimes seeing jail time. They saw the error of their ways when Major Leavy and the other senior regimental officers heard about it after we returned. I was walking the tight rope, of staying within the law while participating in group activities. My only problem was as I learned my new vehicle, the 75 Dodge Coronet, was staying out of the OPP's radar. As I drove back and forth between CFB Petawawa and my home in the Ottawa area, inevitably police were waiting in ambush. I remember getting a few speeding tickets, but avoided more serious offences that year.

The Army for the most part kept me on the right path, my focus being to be a solid Airborne paratrooper, passing the series of tasks and Performance Objectives. Everything we did as young soldiers was recorded, going into our Personal Files. This affected our future in the Armed Forces, from resigning and retention (or release) and promotions and courses. That fall in October I was assigned to the Machine Gun Course for advanced training. In June, I had completed my first infantry qualification, the TQ 4 Qualification. For the next year, I was completing my next qualification, TQ 5 Infantry. This I completed in June 26, 1985. The MG course was part of this, which I successfully completed and received my certificate on 9 November 1984. I told the course officer Lt. Beaudette later and the CO Major Bragdon (2 AB CDO) that it was a basic refresher for me. I had passed the M.G. course already, had in fact instructed the course, prior to being posted to The Airborne Regiment. It did not change much and I had to repeat the course. I passed it easily of course, the focus being on the 7.62 mm GPMG and .50 Calibre HMG. There were lessons in tents on the Mattawa Plain, followed by strip and assembly, operating drills, followed by live fire on ranges. Both weapons were developed by the U.S. Army dating back to W.W. 2 and purchased for the Canadian Army. Both were discontinued after I left the Army in 1987. So, in that month I was recognized as a trained Airborne rifleman and machine gunner.

I also qualified in a wide range of other activities. I frequently threw live grenades on a separate range and rappelled off a tower to practice rappelling off Huey choppers. This I mentioned earlier was used during Mountain school to get down steep cliffs quickly. Winter Battle School which took place every winter, included using live grenades (while assaulting enemy bunkers, trenches and vehicles), platoon snow defences, section attacks (8-10 men), live fire "bush lanes", using Nordic skis, snowshoes, and using/blowing up AFV (enemy armoured vehicles). A special advanced course taught me to use various means in destroying enemy vehicles. From basic 'Molotov cocktails', IED's, mines, boobytraps (using fused explosives and C-4 plastic explosives I was becoming an increasingly highly trained threat to any enemy I might come up against. Also in October, I participated in an unusual course, termed Ex. Trial Chase. I believe it was to train the medical staff in treating real battle casualties in future armed conflicts, which were in the not to distant future. So, I was playing a simulated battle casualty, with various wounds. The casualties were evacuated from where we were taking part in a field tactical exercise, to the base hospital in ambulances. Other soldiers bandaged our 'simulated wounds' then loaded us onto stretchers, each wounded soldier tagged for a level of treatment. I took a nonchalant 'cavalier' approach to that exercise. It was easy, no heavy physical activity, just lie on an exam table and have nurses poke and prod your body. I joked with the prettier nurses, assuring them I would pull through and would be available for dates later. They took it in their stride, almost expecting my proposal, while the sterner doctors frowned at my effrontery!

However, before Ex. Trial Chase II concluded on October 4, I learned real, serious lessons as a simulated battle casualty. How I looked at medical staff, their professional approach to treating me should I be injured, enabled myself in dealing with actual injuries. This I would experience later, some being life threatening or possible loss of limbs. Also as part of my continuation training, I took part in several parachute drops that fall. In October I did two jumps, two more in November and one in December. These were all on DZ Anzio in Petawawa, the Airborne's home base. The October jumps were easy, being daylight administrative 'non-tactical' drops, on the 20th and 24th. I was slotted in at #3 and 4 port stick, consecutively on the C-130Hercules from the side doors.

On November 1, I jumped from the side door again on the C-130 at #12 starboard stick. This was a bit more challenging, with full equipment and at night. On November 22, I jumped from an American C141 Starlifter for the first time, at #6 Port side. This plane is to this day, the largest jump aircraft in the world, with four twin-turbo jet engines and can carry a massive payload. It can carry nearly 200 paratroopers and up to three heavy armoured vehicles, which drop from the rear ramp. So about three or four were needed to drop our entire Airborne Regiment, one Commando company in each plane, with all of our weapons, equipment and vehicles! As I waited for the green light, the American crew chief joked about not exiting too hard, or our main chutes would be shredded by the jet exhaust out in front of the door! We looked at him dubiously, trying to discern whether he was joking or not. But we took it seriously, our usual shouts of Airborne and dirty jokes falling silent. But in the end, we exited as usual, pulling it off without a single chute being turned into ashes! On December 7, we did the final jump of the year, my 26th overall. It was back to the Herc C-130, where I was #6 port side again. It was a tactical full equipment drop during Exercise Pegasus Strike.

All of these drops went perfect from my perspective, no injuries or other nasty things occurred. It was cold though as I floated to Earth, looking around I saw the long lines of chutes around me, some 180 paratroopers floating over the snow-covered ground below. I was feeling growing confidence in my ability to handle these drops, then performing on the ground after. Physically I was in prime condition, handling loads of over 100 pounds, then marching for days with minimal rest. Mentally it was important to show the boss, one could not only handle it, but display a cool, aggressive and esprit-de-corps attitude. Speed of movement, expertise in accomplishing any task assigned to us, communication verbally or on radios, everything was noted and recorded later in our personal records. This exercise was basically a warm up for the more challenging winter exercises soon to follow in early 1985. After landing on Anzio, it was a flurry of activity, bundling up our parachutes, donning gear and rushing to the RV's. Then re-organized into our units, received orders and marched off the DZ. The important point here was to clear the DZ ASAP, as in a real situation it could be in close proximity of the enemy and every second counted. The strength of any unit is only as good as the weakest, slowest man, so our leaders frowned on any weakness and tried to eliminate them.

After the exercise concluded and we had marched back on base, my platoon and myself grinned and slapped each other in high spirits. We 'got 'er done' and had not lost a man. The year concluded after doing administrative work, countless weapons maintenance and inspections and daily physical training. At last we went on Christmas holidays, about two weeks, before returning to work in the first week of January 1985. Warrant Palmer our newest platoon 2 I/C had a final word to our platoon.

"Good job fellahs. Enjoy your leave but be ready to haul ass in January...and don't be late! January 3rd or bust. On parade ready for morning PT or it's jail for you! Airborne!"

"Airborne! Hell Ya!" We replied in a shouted chorus, then sprinted for the barracks as if our very lives depended on us getting off base in the next few minutes. After a shower and packing I jumped in my Dodge Coronet and exited the base for Ottawa. I made it in record time to Ottawa and was soon celebrating in Molly McGuire's Irish pub that night with many other Airborne and one of my new girl friends. The night was filled with cheerful, drunken debauchery, as usual, maybe a few fights just to keep us sharp! But being a good lad, I left before anything nasty happened with my adoring sweetheart in tow. I tried to keep the 'shop talk' and war stories to a minimum, focussing on our relationship, taking my mind off the Army. I spent the last few weeks of 1984 in the Ottawa area and visiting my ancestral home near Plantagenet, on the Nation River, 60 kilometers east of the capital. The house and farmland, about 100 acres had been in my ancestor's hands for the previous two centuries.

After the Christmas holidays were over I rejoined my girl friend in Ottawa where we made the rounds, attending several festive occasions, concluded with New Years Eve. Then in early January I said good-bye to her and loading up my car drove back to Petawawa. Back on base, I carried my gear inside 3 Commando barracks. That night joined by several platoon mates, I went to the Airborne drinking mess. Over a few beers, we happily discussed our leave and the next phase of our training.

Early next morning, dressed in PT gear, we were greeted by the CSM and the Co Major Leavy. Formed up in ranks we shivered in the chilling bitter wind as we were told to get ready for upcoming Winter Warfare. Over the next half-year, I would complete the numerous performance objectives of the Army TQ-5A Qualification. This was signed off by the 3 Commando Adjutant Captain Dodson on the 26th of June, as well as the new CO Major Ring. As we ran down the road that morning, freezing and struggling to breathe in the frigid -20C air I knew it would be a long, busy year.

That January winter training included a series of specific drills, including grenade assaults (live), building platoon defensive positions (using snow and ice blocks), small section attacks, live fire bush lanes, skiing with Nordic skis and using AFV vehicles Mechanized armoured carriers). This phase in training concluded on February 1, basically a refresher for me, now in my tenth year in the Infantry. The only year I did not go through winter warfare was the upcoming 6 month U.N. tour in Cyprus. This would see 3 Commando flown to the Mediterranean island in August, not returning to Canada until the following February. In February 1985, it was back to parachuting, completing two (#27, 28) on the 21st and 26th respectively. Both were from Hercules C-130s, the first being a night full equipment jump, also for the first time I was No. 1, the port stick leader.

"Finally! I am first out the door, setting the table." As the jump master opened the door and did the preliminary checks, I could look out at the black void awaiting us. It was an adrenaline rush for a young paratrooper as I waited for the red light to turn green. "This is nothing, nothing at all!" I reassured myself, for there was no live fire arcing up toward the plane from the ground, unlike during WW 2. I knew of the German attack on the island of Crete in 1941, the largest German Falchirmjagger (Airborne) drop of the war. In the debacle that followed, thousands of German paratroopers were slaughtered, by the Allied defenders, many dead before they even left the Junkers transports, or shot while drifting down under their chutes. Then there was the Allied drop on D-Day (June 6th), Operation Market Garden in Holland (Sept.1944) and Operation Varsity (March 1945).

With the blissful thoughts of these live combat jumps in my mind, I saw with relief the light blink to green. I shouted Airborne in glee before leaping into the inky blackness. Seconds later I grunted as I felt the sharp tug as the main cracked open. Gasping in icy Arctic air, I blinked focussing my eyes up to check the chute. Relieved as it billowed open, I saw the Herc's big dark fuselage above, disgorging the two sticks of my Airborne brothers in quick succession. We jumped at around 800 feet, so as I looked below my mukluk boots, I saw the dark, snow covered ground rising rapidly. Hurriedly I went through the drills in flight, finally releasing my gear below 50 feet.

Bracing to touch down on Mother earth, I tucked my chin down on my chest, feet and knees together, slightly bent. My gloved hands gripped the overhead risers, telling myself sub-consciously, "Relax, relax...a piece of cake." Then I hit, rolled and struggled to rise from the snow. The adrenaline still pumped, as I stood watching as hundreds of chutes drifted above, then rapidly and almost silently 3 Commando dropped all around me.

Five days later we jumped again, on DZ Anzio, concluding Winter Warfare Ops for the year. It was an administrative equipment jump in the daylight. I was #15 port side on the C-130 and was a routine, unremarkable jump. As I dropped my gear at the Commando Rv minutes later, I saw Sergeant Scotty Collins, our veteran DZ Controller peering intently at me.

"Trooper Gilligan, good job. How many jumps is that son?" I nodded to him, replying 28 as I deposited my chute at his feet. "Nice work Trooper. Wait till next month. We will be jumping into the Texas desert!" I shouted Airborne in response, then jogged off with my gear to 10 Platoon's Rv. Ernie Hall was now my section I/C, standing like a silent Greek statue in the snow as his guys jogged in. "10Platoon here guys. My section line up here." Ernie was a cool NCO, nothing fazed him that I ever saw. Calmly he inspected us and our gear, walking slowly down the line. Soon after we marched off the snow covered DZ toward the distant base, our mukluks sinking into the snow drifts. I tucked my chin into the collar of my Arctic parka, grilling myself for the long march back to the main camp. An hour or so later we arrived at the weapons stores compound. We gratefully dumped our gear, most of us lighting up cigarettes and swilling water from our canteens. We spent the rest of the morning cleaning our weapons before turning them in the QM staff, along with any ammunition and pyrotechnics.

Major Leavy met us on parade that afternoon on the Airborne parade square to debrief us. Nearby 1 and 2 Commando also held a parade before weekend leave. The CO did not mince words with us, "Men good job, winter battle school is over. Most of you have the weekend off, at the discretion of your platoon sergeant. Next week we get ready for Texas and desert training. So, enjoy the time off and party hard. Airborne! CSM take over." Sergeant Major Irvine saluted as the CO departed along with the rest of the officers, leaving the company to the NCO's. After getting info on the next week's timings, the men of 3 Commando were dismissed. It went like a drill by now, rush to the barracks, shower, change to civvy clothes, then to the eating mess. On Friday, it was usually something edible, like steak, onions and spuds.

The veteran guys skipped this, the married ones soon at home off the base or in the PMQ's (married quarters). Others went to the various drinking messes to start drinking and getting in a mood to party the night away. Others like myself, who could drive and owned vehicles, were soon headed off base to distant locales.

For myself, that was Ottawa and its environs. There I met my new girl friend, Suzy Q. from Newfoundland. It had taken allot of legwork to convince her I was worthy of her time. Fortunately, her cousin also from Newfie land, Brian Keefe, who was in the Airborne's Pathfinder platoon and I got along. Perhaps he put in a good word for me to Suzy. So finally, we were dating regularly, then had the big meeting with her parents. Invited to their house I met Mr. Keefe, who turned out to be an officer in the Canadian Forces. We got along fine, all were pleased to meet me, a young paratrooper.

Suzy was nice I guess, but a bit cold and slow to commit to anything that did not offer her any visible, if not financial gain. At least that is how I remember her years later. That first night I spent at her parent's house in Quebec, it was a dubious affair. Being old fashioned, we stayed apart, not even a good night kiss and slept in separate bedrooms. She saw me come out the next morning, heading for the washroom. I was not wearing a shirt, sending her into a frenzy, admonishing me for being so casual in Her parent's house. It left me with a bleak view of our relationship going far into the future. Otherwise it was a great weekend in Ottawa, escorted about town by my latest girl. Suzy was very intelligent, being a university student.

She was not a cheap date though. When I arrived back on base that Sunday night, I was a bit lighter in my wallet. In those days of no debit cards or cell phones, or personal computers for that matter, things were simpler. Before going on leave, withdraw all your money from the base pay officer, then spend it all before returning to work. Then start all over again! I had yet to learn the fine art of balancing a check book. In fact I wrote very few checks and had no credit at the time. Besides I was in a dangerous business, being a Canadian warrior, training for battle I lived from one day to the next, aware that every day could be my last. Who had time to plan for the future?

In hindsight, knowing what I know now, I would have planned better. Being young and in the 1980's all my efforts went into the short term. I was focussed on being a professional soldier, everything else was secondary. I moved in the military world, then becoming a paratrooper, a circle within a circle. Like my Airborne buddies, we rarely talked or associated with civilians, other than girlfriends, wives and family. Like today, as a civilian skydiver, most of my inner circle are other skydivers, men and women. I have tried to talk to non-jumpers over the years, finding it frustrating as they show no interest in anything as dangerous as this sport. I actually have become comfortable with this now, as it eliminates allot of people from my life, who have little if any of my interests. Anyone who thinks it is crazy to jump from an airplane, I do not want to hang out with. One or two good friends I can trust are better than a hundred people I can not trust or relate to. Canadians hate the word elite, because they are not.

    Most Canadians I know prefer a more mundane, safe and non-risk lifestyle. Canadian society is trying to alienate our past and create an image as a non-violent, pacifistic and non-threatening nation. This was the primary reason why The Airborne Regiment was disbanded in the 1990's. Now a trained paratrooper infantryman, in 1985 it was time to show the world what I could do, along with my Commando and platoon mates. What mattered most to us, was being rated by our peers in the Elite Special Forces of our Western Allies and being respected and feared by our enemies abroad. Well Canada was never attacked so this speaks for itself.

Foreign Service

The Canadian Airborne Regiment was the SSF's core unit, tasked with primarily the defence of Canada, particularly the far north and the sparsely populated Arctic Islands. Secondly, we had to be prepared for action anywhere in the world, and on short notice. In effect, we were the nucleus of the future Special Forces, based on the first lessons learned during WW 2. To deal with the newest threat, terrorists mostly from the Middle East, we were trained in small unit tactics, behind-the lines work, Escape & Evasion, snatch & grab exercises and hostage rescue. After returning to Petawawa the following week, we packed and left for Ottawa's International Airport. We boarded Boeing airliners for the long flight south to Texas. It was early March, so we were overjoyed to leave the last days of winter behind. In exchange for the sub-zero temperatures, snow and ice we landed in El Paso's simmering heat.

Within hours of landing, the entire regiment was in the desert. Dressed in our olive drab combat uniforms, we unpacked and began erecting our standard field tents. I remember looking over the desert at the 2 Commando lines, who were situated next to 3 Commando. There fluttering in the breeze was their unofficial battle flag, the old Confederate flag. I smiled at my buddy McGean. "Hey dude, check it out! 2 Commando...what a bunch of pricks!"

"Ya here have a butt. Let's get acclimatized eh?" I laughed at his joke and lit up the cigarette, sitting in the hot sand next to the hole. Brian was one of my closest friends, from Cape Breton. We had spent the last two years in the same platoon, enduring the same brutal training and parachute jumps. I trusted him like a brother, along with about a dozen others, all by now experienced paratroopers. As we smoked, our eyes slitted against the blazing overhead sun, one eye on alert for preying Senior NCO's. The new ones were the worst as we knew, eager to make their names known to the officers. "Fucking brown nosers! That new guy in 12 Platoon is the worst. Got his nose so far up the Captain's ass he needs a snorkel!" We laughed ourselves horse, cutting down the poor NCO dude's tattered reputation, in the manner of all lower rank soldiers worldwide.

After finishing setting up our desert base camp, we were served dinner at the newly erected field eating mess. Much to our surprise the grub was not that bad either. To heighten our spirits even more, the CSM announced the wet mess and bar would be open soon.

"Enjoy a beer or two lads. Tomorrow we start earning our pay. The Yanks have advised us to take it easy for a few days and acclimatize to this heat. The Major wants to teach them a lesson about Airborne. We will do a hump through the desert, full battle dress and rucks." We responded with an enthusiastic Airborne "Hell Ya!" After a quick meal, I followed the crowd to the nearby tent housing the new bar. I can tell y'all for nothing, there is little better than cold beer after sweating in the desert all day. The last thing on our minds was the upcoming hump early the next day. For most of us, the desert was a new thing, so why worry about it? Enjoy the moment. We had an old saying then, "Travel to foreign exotic lands, meet Exotic people and kill 'em all!" As we sang songs, drank cold Coors beer and initiated our new FNG's (new guys), all was good. Finally, after midnight we were kicked out, under the threat by the Mess officer the bar would stay closed if we did not play nice. We returned to our tents, staggering across the dark desert, uttering departing insults to the mess crew. Fatigued as we were, we did not fall asleep till much later. We told war stories, chain smoked and drank from a few looted bottles.

The next morning: It was the first week of March as I stood in the ranks of 10 Platoon. For this desert operation, the platoon was under strength, with about 26 men. This was of course not unusual in the Canadian

Forces since I had enlisted. Also, we had temporarily attached personnel (two reservists and a medic). It was early morning in our desert camp as the platoon officer and our newly appointed Warrant Officer Palmer addressed the men.

We wore our combat uniforms, combat boots and field hats as the desert sun beat down on or heads. Nearby placed in a line before our olive drab tents, lay our combat gear, rucksacks and weapons. 2nd Lieutenant Patchet gave us a morning briefing then turned over the parade to Warrant Palmer, saluted and strolled off to talk with the 3 Commando HQ.

"10 Platoon! Stand easy. Its our first day here in the Texas desert guys. We are just north of El Paso. So, we just concluded Winter warfare. We have a few guys injured so they are back in Petawawa recovering. Two men are on the Pathfinder course. We welcome the new fellahs, our medic and the two militia lads." We grinned over at the new members, knowing they would be under some pressure to fit in, to meet the exacting standards of our tight paratrooper outfit. "Good luck" we muttered as we joked quietly.

"First order of business. Major Leavy has planned a rucksack march to get us acclimatized to the new environment here in the desert. For many of us, this is a new deal. We will have medical safety vehicles in the rear of the Commando. It will take up most of the day, so drink plenty of water. Section commanders inspect your men before we head off. Canteens and the issued desert water containers are full. Weapons check, no rounds loaded. This is the warm up for the upcoming jumps and exercises. The first will be at a DZ Coors in Texas, full equipment, tactical platoon exercise. Our taxi will be the trusty C-130. The second jump will be at the same DZ, equipment but administrative, non-tactical. These will get the Regiment ready for the main exercise Border Star. This will be in about two weeks somewhere in New Mexico, the next state over to the west. Men we are under a microscope here, the American Army is listening and watching. We will be the Enemy Force for the 10th Light Mountain Division. The Regiment with attached Battle Group elements from the 8th CH (armour), HQ & Signals, Combat Engineers and E Battery RCHA will number 800 paratroopers. Our foe numbers over 15000, including their armour and attached Air Force. So, as you can see, we have our work cut out for us. The OC expects each of us to give our best effort. Take care what you say and how you conduct yourselves when Americans or the press are present. If any media ask for a comment, you will refer them to our press officer. Right questions?"

10 Platoon stood silent as we absorbed this information. No one said a word, then it was time to gear up for the big Commando rucksack march. We walked over to gather up our gear, donning combat webbing, shouldering rucksacks, shifting the heavy loads to the best fit. Plunking on my steel helmet, I bent over and

picked up my personal rifle, the FN C1 semi-automatic 7.62mm standard issue rifle in the Canadian Army. Then led by Master Corporal Ernie Hall, my section's I/C, he gave us some last-minute instructions.

"Ok guys, you know the drill. For you new guys, keep it tight. No talking, follow on the heels of the guy in front. OK form up in platoon files. Jump up and down! Tighten any loose gear, when we start there will be no time. No one falls out...got me?" We nodded silently, considering the NCO's dark slitted eyes. Shortly after, Major Leavy gave the march order and we trudged off into the vast expanse of the Texas desert. It was another day at the office for me, adjusting my pace leaning forward, head bent down, my mind went into neutral. As a trained, veteran infantryman I knew how to handle these humps. Ignore the outside world, the steady, monotonous slog through the hot sand. All I saw was the few soldiers plodding ahead of me, the sound of vehicle engines following us in the rear. There was something like 100 men on the march in 3 Commando that long, hot day. A few American advisors had joined us to advise and take note of our performance. I heard they had recommended that the Airborne not attempt any long marches this soon after our arrival, which fell on deaf ears of course.

It was like what I knew the 1st Special Service Force had done in Montana, when the first Canadian-American Commando unit started their training in 1942. One of the precursors to the Canadian Airborne Regiment, along with 1st Canadian Parachute Battalion, we modern day paratroopers took great pride in carrying on the success and traditions of our valiant predecessors. So as tough and exhausting as it was, sweating out our bodies, 3 Commando trudged back into our desert base camp hours later. To the surprise of our Yankee counterparts, I do not believe we lost a man. That means we not only survived that blistering hell, no man fell out of ranks. The Bear was pleased of course, probably gloating as he told the American advisors attached to the HQ. I gasped in relief, dropping my sweat soaked gear before my tent. I unclipped the helmet strap, tilting it back on my head, then dug my cigarettes out of my combat shirt pocket, simultaneously uncorking my desert canteen. I sucked back my first cool water in hours, easing my burning throat. Sweat stung my eyes as I lit up a cigarette, inhaling with pleasure, feeling a sort of rush go though my body and mind. I felt like I was almost floating over the desert sand, relieved of the 80 odd pounds of weapons and gear I had humped for around 25 miles. I was in top physical condition, but had probably shed close to 10 pounds during my first desert march. "March or croak guys! Airborne...hell-ya!" We had yelled mile after mile, encouraging each other.

After a few minutes to relax, it was back to our field routine. Another of the endless weapons checks, cleaning and inspections. Routine O-groups informed us of the next thing, the next hurdle to be leaped. It was a good start though, as quickly we eased into the desert routine, one thing at a time. Next on the agenda for 3 Commando was a short two-day field exercise from March 7 to 9. We moved to Fort Bliss, Texas for Ex. Nimrod Caper. I was at this time a rifleman in 10 Platoon. M/Cpl. Hall was the section commander, a cool headed, experienced NCO and Airborne soldier. This exercise we practised small unit procedures in the desert. Advance to contact, deliberate assaults, camouflage and concealment, patrolling and radio comms. Like any good infantry unit, we drilled in our procedures over and over, till it became second nature to us. We became familiar with every man in our teams of maneuver, our weapons and equipment. As we trained in this desert environment we grew in confidence, knowing we could achieve any objective handed to us.

The period from March 10-21, entailed constant platoon level training. On March 13, we did our first parachute descent onto DZ Coors. I was #10 Portside stick in the Hercules. This was our tactical platoon exercise, to warm up for the bigger follow up Ops. to come. It went off well, then 10 Platoon practiced exiting the DZ in small units, camouflage and concealment, noise discipline, casualty evacuation and the like. It was more to get the new FNG's accustomed to these drills. But it also helped hone our platoon into a tight, efficient team. For us veterans, who formed the nucleus of the platoon, being together now for nearly two years, we showed our cool confidence and paratrooper esprit-de-corps to the younger troopers. This was emphasized by our officers, frequently junior ranks leading patrols, issuing marching orders and taking over during simulated attacks. It was drilled into us over and over. Every man had to know the mission objectives, in case our leaders were dead, wounded or captured. In actual combat, it was frequently a low-ranking soldier who led his unit to the ultimate objective and success. After a day trekking around in the desert, the far-flung platoons contacted base by radio and were picked up by US Army 5 ton trucks.

The next day 3 Commando parachuted onto DZ Coors, Fort Bliss for the second time, I stood #9 starboard stick inside the bucking C-130. This would be jump #30 for me, relieved as the green light blinked on, the sweating shouting paratroopers surging forward together. In seconds, we had emptied the plane, like a well-oiled machine. I gasped as I felt the cool air on my sweating skin, a relief from the stifling hot, noisy interior of the big transport, which roared away overhead of my CT-1 round chute. I looked down at the vast desert expanse, surrounded by scores of other chutes. I breathed easily, enjoying the moment. This was easy I thought, non-tactical. So probably pack up and a ride back to camp. I released my gear below me as I got ready for the landing. I thumped down into the sand, rolling to absorb the impact.

I gave the thumbs up to some paratroopers standing nearby, then packed my chute and gathered up my gear, then trotted off to the platoon RV 100 meters off. My 30th parachute drop had gone off as planned, so that night we had a little celebration. The OC opened the wet mess for a few cold ones, we were in a high state of morale. We forgot about the demands on us as we relaxed in true Airborne fashion. We discussed the desert training so far, the jumps and sang filthy army songs as we swilled the cold Coors beer from cans. We felt like in another world then, isolated from home, family and Petawawa base camp. I felt then, we were ready for combat, whoever we faced, we would crush them under out boots!

That night as I lay inside the tent on my air mattress, striped down for the night, I dreamed of being in my first, real live combat. I strived to follow in the footsteps of my ancestors, who had fought in the world wars and Korea. It was a life long pursuit of a warrior's life. I believe my descendants, who came from Ireland had Viking blood. Knowing vaguely of their history, a warrior embraced the life, the hardships and preyed for a valiant death in battle. It was the final step to arriving in Valhalla, home of the gods and brave, valiant warriors. As I grew and matured as a soldier, it was a mental game I played. What happened to you after you were dead, was there an afterlife? After a series of near misses with death, I began to joke about being a demi-god, I could not die. I was not alone in this, one of my NCO leaders Mac McDonald also had a few near-death experiences. I looked at him as an immortal warrior.

I also had thoughts of my sweetheart, safe back in Ottawa awaiting my return from foreign locales. As I was engaged in the huge desert operation in Texas, I assured myself of my duty. Protect Canada first and foremost, so my loved ones would remain safe at home. It would have been the goal of every soldier going back centuries, to the brave 300 Spartan warriors at Thermopylae. They like the Vikings, Roman centurions and legions of armies after, fought and died to protect their homeland and loved ones. Then there was Achilles, the famed Greek demigod, who fought to become immortalized while fighting in the Trojan war. As I slept that night and many a night after, I wondered what the gods and the future held for myself and my mates.

For the next two weeks, the Airborne Regiment continued to fine tune our desert warfare skills. One day while we practiced our skill at camouflage and concealment, our American advisors advised us to stay away from small sand hillocks. "We have rattlesnakes here, they like to hide in these dunes and mounds. This caught our full attention, our ears perking up at the mention of the deadly venomous snakes. Shortly afterward, we bagged our first kill. Sergeant Scotty Collins, a legend and one of the oldest original members of the Airborne Regiment, caught the hissing rattler. He held it in one hand up to our Platoon Commander, 2nd Lt. Patchet. "Here ya go Sir! Ha-ha! Take it!"

He held the twisting huge rattlesnake behind its open jaws, its rattlers going off like a siren! The young officer I heard later ran off in horror, then Scotty took a machete and lopped off its head. Later after skinning it, he cooked it over a bon fire. We laughed and joked as we added snake meat to our hard rations at dinner. We called it living off the land. As we were trained in survival skills and Escape Evasion, we knew living off the land's sometime meager resources was an essential skill to living or death.

Later our trusted section I/C M/Cpl Ernie Hall went snake hunting, while the rest of the platoon was on leave in the city of El Paso. We were surprised he had declined to join us after weeks out in the desert. But when we returned two days later, he presented each of his section soldiers a snake headband to attach to our head gear as a souvenir. Another part of the local fauna we got to know was the horny desert lizard. It was Larry LeClair who was entertaining us one evening with his guitar at one of our frequent bon fires. One trooper spotted it lunching on one of our ration packs. We gathered around examining the lizard as it sat placidly in the hand of Larry. We laughed as we poked, prodded and fed it our rations. It was about a hand length long and clearly not a threat, its snake like tongue licking the rations to suck out moisture we thought. We took to the lizard immediately, adorning it as our Texas desert mascot. Larry the Lizard followed us around for the rest of our desert stay, jumping in with us in the big final exercise and the days that followed. It was all on our mind by now, Exercise Border Star.

March 22: Still at Fort Bliss, Exercise Bear Claw III was our next unit exercise. This was the last warm-up for the big final exercise in our desert operation. It was a bigger company level exercise, most likely to give Major Leavy's 3 Commando HQ the chance to exercise command and control of our four platoons. All I remember personally was endless marches, mostly at night. It drew on each man's reserves of strength and endurance, as we plodded through the vast desert expanses. One could see the far-off lights of the base, which never seemed to get closer as hour after hour we plodded along loaded to the hilt with our gear. This exercise concluded on March 25, then it was back to base. There over the next day we got ready for Exercise Border Star. We spent the hectic hours drawing parachute rigs, rigging up our rucksacks and weapons. In our gear, we packed a week's worth of rations and ammunition. Additional gear including pyrotechnics, radio batteries, anti-tank weapons (M-72, Carl Gustav rocket launchers, C-4 explosive for IED's) were given to us depending on our strengths. A few lucky ones also got to carry mortar bombs for our 60 mm and 81 mm mortars.

March 27: The big day had arrived, as we dressed for the jump in a hangar on Fort Bliss. Outside long lines of aircraft assembled on the taxi airstrip. Most were our standard C-130 Hercules, the aircrews going through their take-off procedures, revving up the four huge engines, testing brakes and flaps. Unseen to us and the Yankee enemy, our Pathfinders had already parachuted into the area where we would parachute into. Pathfinders were always first in, doing reconnaissance and choosing the drop zones, then mounting security patrols. This would show its importance in the next few hours, for it was vital the enemy did not locate these drop zones as we landed. It was at this point that Airborne units were at there weakest. This was displayed clearly in the September 1944 Operation Market Garden. The Germans had discerned at an early stage were the DZ's were and the objective, Arnhem Bridge. The British 1st Airborne Division payed the supreme price, losing close to 10,000 men killed, wounded or captured. In my European deployments, I had visited their grave sites in Holland. Standing in those beautifully preserved cemeteries, it hit me hard. These men, young soldiers like myself had sacrificed their lives decades before I was born to defeat evil and tyranny.

    Finally, after we had donned our parachute harness, attached rucks and weapons, we were inspected by our jump masters. It was routine for every jump, checking each part of our gear from combat boots to our steel helmets. We groaned under the back-breaking weight, as the JM's tugged on harness straps, then slapped our back. "Your OK jumper!" Then we sat down on long benches as night approached. We relaxed and many lit up cigarettes, talking and joking light heartedly. The Bear Leavy and the officers made their rounds through the crowded hangar, studying maps and going over the latest DZ info from the Pathfinders. In essence we were briefed there would be two DZs, a primary and an alternate. In the case where the primary DZ was compromised, i.e. the enemy had located and occupied it, we would be diverted to the second alternate DZ. For it was vital in the first hour or so, that we organize into our platoons and get off the DZ before the Yanks knew where we were. Otherwise they would have us "in the bag" and it was game over. For the odds were stacked against us, at least 15:1!

This was I knew no ordinary parachute jump, my 31st in my career. I was 27 years old at the time and consoled myself as I sat waiting that I had demonstrated my ability to handle it. This waiting period was the worst, as thoughts went through one's head about how it would unfold. Not being in a leadership position then, I knew my main task would be as part of a large team of some 800 Canadian paratroopers to land on the DZ and get to 3 Commando's RV, in the pitch blackness of the desert. Silence and speed were crucial…and not get injured! As we received our final briefing, we were given a compass and direction to get to it. Also, each RV was marked by the DZ Pathfinders by a coloured, blinking beacon.

Finally, after midnight we got the go, getting up I followed the long line of my stick to the waiting Hercules outside. It was a long, painstaking walk, burdened with over 100 pounds of gear, up the rear ramp to our seats in the dimly lit cabin. I was slotted in at #7 port side, the JM's checking our names and ensuring proper order. I sank heavily onto the nylon seat, the crushing weight of my rig and attached gear pressing my body into the seat like a vice. I tilted my steel helmet up, wiping the sweat from my forehead. "Well here we are guys. Can we smoke?" Shortly after the Herc crew chief raised the rear ramp and gave the OK for the pilot in the forward cabin to taxi off to the take off point. The Hercules rumbled down the taxi lane, following a long line of some 24 C-130's, then we heard the engines rev up to full power. After several minutes, I felt the breaks release, then the plane surged forward into the night. It was game time, feeling the telltale lurch as we lifted off into the desert air.

It was a long flight of several hours, the DZ being in New Mexico to the west. I was in a dazed state as I sat there in the dark, noisy fuselage cabin, one of some sixty odd paratroopers. Each of us was in his own world and thoughts, thinking of home and loved ones. Some preyed to our God, hoping to emerge from this dangerous world in one piece! Some of the newer guys experienced air sickness, the plane rocking and jolting in the turbulent currents as we flew low over the desert terrain to avoid radar. We paratroopers had our lives in the hands of the pilots, trusting they were the best in the world at flying a huge, heavily laden aircraft. We all knew that any aircraft flight had inherent risks, but this took it to a new level. For it was a one-way trip, if it went to plan, the Hercs would return to base after disgorging it's load of paratroopers.

It was the full meal deal, a nighttime, full equipment, tactical jump. At last we were nearing the primary DZ sometime around 02:30 A.M. The JM's shouted stand up, hook up. Releasing our seatbelts, we struggled to stand up in the bucking aircraft. It took all my strength to stand, then grabbing the static line looped on my belly reserve, reach up and clip it on the overhead cable. I went over my harness with one hand, checking my helmet straps were fastened securely, then waited for the standard JM safety check. The two JM's slowly made their way down the long lines of the port and starboard sticks, carefully checking equipment and static line. Finally, all was ready, the doors opened and the Herc crew checked all was ready. I looked out the port side window, seeing only inky blackness outside. There were no lights, for this was in the middle of New Mexico's desert. It being tactical, typically I knew we would jump at below a 1000 feet. Not much time in the air to enjoy the view.

I heard the 10-minute warning, the adrenaline screaming through my veins, knowing in the next few minutes I would be exiting the speeding Herc to the inky blackness outside. The red light blinked on the door, the chants of Airborne echoing in the cabin as the JM's and aircrew grinned at each other. The number 1's were braced in the door now, the JM next to them, one hand extended in front. Then the shout came..." Stop drop!" We gasped as we took it in, what had happened? I cursed softly, as we then unhooked and sat back down. As it turned out, the Pathfinder DZ crew down below had alerted the C-130 pilots that our main DZ was compromised! Some how, our enemy the Yanks of the 10th Light Mountain Division had learned where our primary DZ was and were waiting on the ground for us. If not for the vigilance of the elite Pathfinders, our operation would have ended in a very sudden failure.

It was disappointing at the time, but soon after we were told we would be landing at our alternate DZ in about a half hour. It was termed DZ Desperado, located several miles away, presumably still in New Mexico. Again, we stood up about fifteen minutes before arriving, hooking up again and awaiting the word. At last it came, the green light blinking on! My left hand gripped the sling of my FNC1 strapped to my shoulder, the right fiercely gripping the static line over my head. My eyes focussed on the door ahead, the JM gathering the static lines as rapidly the six jumpers ahead of me jumped out the door. In seconds it was my turn, throwing the static line forward, I pivoted left into the door, then jabbed out into the night. Mentally I counted to four as I was thrashed about in the turbulent wash of the big engines. It was exciting and thoroughly crazy, being jerked sideways by the static line as it yanked out my chute. To any sane person, it would have been hell. Why jump from a perfectly serviceable airplane?

"Because...we are Airborne!" That was always my first response, the elite of the Canadian Army, first in, last out in battle. I felt the sharp tug on my harness, looking up to see the big round CT-1 main parachute billow open overhead. It was a feeling of joy and relief, knowing I would probably survive the night! Then it was back to business, surveying my immediate surroundings for other chutes. The chance of a mid air collision was always present with hundreds of chutes in the air at once. We had been schooled on this during Basic Para, then during yearly refresher courses. Never let your guard down, constant alertness. The closest jumper to me was some dozen meters away, swinging to and fro like myself.

"Slip away!" I shouted to him, tugging on my risers to separate us. I looked down at my boots, just making out the ground, probably around 500 feet below. I tugged on the waist strap, releasing my weapon shoulder load. Holding my rifle by the sling, I felt under the reserve for the two quick releases. Finding them I waited till I was below 100 feet or so, glanced around one more time, seeing dozens of chutes, some just landing below. Then I hit the quick releases, dropping my heavy ruck and weapon below. I kicked the nylon cord tied to my webbing, the load swinging below to drop on the ground first. I saw the blinking lights of the RV points some distance away, the next stop on my late-night journey. I braced for the landing, trying to relax and land safely. I heard the load hit, then bending my knees, feet together, my hands gripping the overhead risers, chin tucked firmly into my chest. I hit the desert sand, rolling to absorb the impact. A few seconds later, I stood up gasping but unhurt, the adrenaline still pumping along with my heart rate. It was no time to celebrate though, as quickly we bundled our chutes into the attached nylon carry bag and donned our rucksacks. I detached my FNC1 from the rigging line, attached a loaded magazine and cocked the lever, loading a 7.62 mm round into the breech. I checked the weapon was on safe, then checked my compass, the heading already set, I marched off to the blinking DZ beacon off in the distance.

I heard someone screaming off in the distance, thinking someone was not having a great night. It turned out one of my platoon mates had the unfortunate luck to land on a rattlesnake. The snake had bitten him, probably scaring the crap out of the unlucky trooper. Fortunately, I heard later, he had been medivacked in time and spent the next few days recuperating in hospital. Finally, around 03:00 A.M. as I looked at the dial of my watch, I dropped off my chute bag in the Commando RV. We spent the next hour or so organizing into our platoons and section teams. Ernie Hall came by, inspecting our gear and asking if we had any problems.

"None to speak of Ernie. What's up next?" We sat in the sand, sneaking a quick gulp of water from our canteens as we waited. Stars twinkled overhead, then I felt the cold as the adrenaline wore off. For those who are desert novices it does get cold, although nothing like what we had experienced in Winter battle school a month before. It was probably around 10 C or slightly less, with a cool breeze. But after the hectic action of the last few hours, I was sweating profusely, so the air felt cold. So it was a relief, when finally 10 Platoon got the word from 3 Commando HQ to head off the DZ. Each of the dozen or so platoons in the Airborne Regiment were given separate objectives that first night, marching off quietly on specific compass headings. We had few vehicles on the DZ, these being reserved for the HQ officers, attached US observers, and heavy equipment. For the average paratrooper, like myself, it was our feet that carried us. Hence it was vital not to get injured on landing.

"Suck it up buttercup!" The standard response to any guy complaining of some minor injury. I don't know how far we marched that first night, but probably over 10 miles. We reached it around first light, carefully observing the target with starlight and binoculars. Slowly our sections maneuvered into attack position, then we struck without further ado. My team ran in screaming Airborne and other battle cries as pyrotechnics exploded. Scrambling over a dune I stood face to face with a large armoured vehicle. I saw no enemy in the vicinity, so scrambled on top of the tracked carrier, probably a M-113 APC. I banged on the closed hatches with the butt of my rifle, hissing, "OK Yanks! You all are my prisoners, get out!" Shortly after the surprised crew emerged, rubbing their eyes after emerging abruptly from their sleep.

As it turned out, our objective was a complete mechanized armoured company of our Yankee foe, the 10th Mountain Division. They had expected that our Airborne force would be captured hours earlier on our main DZ. So, relaxing the guard of course, the company had posted no perimeter sentries. Most were asleep inside their nice warm vehicles. Our twenty odd men captured close to 200 men without a fight. We victoriously stripped the prisoners of state-of the art night vision goggles, weapons and rations. We were told by the confident Americans before the op., that we could do this. Any gear we captured, including vehicles, was ours for the rest of the exercise. This changed shortly after our early success. Umpires in comms with the HQ. informed us we had to return all of our loot. The vehicles were to be written off as destroyed and removed from the exercise which was set for about two weeks.

I was pissed personally, as I handed my Yank prisoner his rifle back. He was a skinny black lad, his eyes showing his fear as this painted devil from Hell probably stood over him. I grinned whispering, "A lesson for you Yank. Never go to sleep around us Canucks from the Great White North. We never sleep on an Op. If you get in combat, keep your guard up. Respect your enemy...and then kill them!" We took a few minutes to regroup, as the officer and umpire consulted on our next move. Then we lit up cigarettes, opened one of two canteens and relaxed. We chatted with the relieved Americans, joking that they would be in the bars before us! For we knew this was just the start, we probably would not be back in "the world" for at least two weeks. As we sat enjoying the brief break, the sun slowly rose over the horizon. Then the radio squawked, "10 Niner this is 3 Niner. Move to grid reference Bravo. Out."

Shortly after 10 Platoon moved out, leaving the captured mechanized company to exit the stage right. After a few miles of marching, we dug in for the day. We were told the Air Force would be out searching for us during the day. Using our entrenching tools, we dug holes in the desert dunes, then camouflaged them. We placed our gear inside, then crawled into the hides. Soon after U.S. Apache, Huey helicopters and A-10 Warthog ground attack aircraft whizzed by overhead. During the daylight hours, our platoon hid in our desert holes, avoiding all contact with our enemy. Then as night approached, we cautiously emerged, packed up and silently marched off to our next objective. The next objective was not nearly as easy as we found out. It was a fluid desert op. the enemy being fully mechanized, the situation changed rapidly. The Airborne enemy being heavily outnumbered, outgunned and on foot, was of course the underdog. So far, we had surprised the 10th Mountain Division. But if they learned our tactics, they could still win a strategic victory.

As in history, war was a foggy, clouded, chaotic mess, where original plans had to be constantly changed to meet mercuric changes as two armies manoeuvered like snakes in a changing landscape. My personal view of the battlefield was a tiny part of the big picture. As part of 10 Platoon, I was a pawn in the big chess game ran miles away. I had experienced this when I was posted to West Germany in 1979. The big NATO exercises there were even bigger than this one, up to 500,000 soldiers in several armies. This was relatively small in comparison, somewhere below 20,000 soldiers and airmen. Primarily Americans in the main Blue force, Canadian Airborne in the enemy "red" force. We were Allies of course, but it was a matter of national and even more important unit pride. We were sent there to learn the art of desert warfare primarily, but to fly the flag as well. We heard the Americans on Fort Bliss looked down with contempt on our puny little Canadian Airborne Regiment. It must have been the same for the million strong Persian Army standing before the Hot Gates at Thermopylae around 300 B.C. There 300 Spartans stood holding the narrow pass in their thin ranks. Behind them the rest of the Greek army cowered in fear, ready to bolt for the rear and safety.

Our other objective in Texas and New Mexico then, was to teach these over confident Americans a lesson. That a small, highly trained force could wreak havoc in the lines of a much bigger, strongly armed force. We had no heavy weapons, artillery, armoured vehicles or supporting air force. We fought with what we carried on our backs, with about enough food, water and ammo to survive for a few days. If we were cornered and in a fierce firefight, our limited resources would quickly evaporate inside an hour or two. So, if we were to survive, never mind win this battle, we relied solely on our wits and cunning. Canadian soldiers of course had gained a reputation over the last century, in adapting to wartime battlefield situations, being constantly aggressive and keeping our enemy off balance. Also, inheriting the British regimental system, the individual grunt was imbued with the spirit of his unit. It was his duty to protect that reputation, the Battle honours, written on the Regimental Flag as if in blood. I had learned this a decade earlier, when as a young recruit infantryman in The Cameron Highlanders of Ottawa, I had watched the Colours marched before my company.

For us Canadian soldiers, it was far better to die in battle than to disgrace the Regimental Flag and Battle honours. This proud tradition had seen Canada through many armed conflicts over the preceding centuries. We boasted an enviable record, we had lost battles but never lost a war. Many had paid the supreme sacrifice, thousands more permanently wounded, but our proud tradition and Canada remained strong. So imbued by this, I was propelled through the desert over the next few days. I learned to conserve my meager rations and water, getting a few moments of shut-eye whenever possible. During the daylight hours as I have said, our primary goal was to remain undetected. I recall peeking out of my camouflaged hole buried into one of the characteristic sand hillocks, seeing Blackhawk and Apache choppers chattering low overhead. If our platoons were spotted, I assume 10th Mountain would have launched air attacks to pin us down. Then mount a sizeable heliborne assault, as A-10 Warthogs strafed us with their payload of 30-mm chain-guns and guided missiles and smart bombs. Long range M-109 mechanized 155 mm artillery and tanks would have shelled us to keep us pinned down.

In live combat, we would have returned fire with our 7.62 mm machine guns, .50 heavy machine guns, mortars, air defence missiles, anti-tank rocket launchers a variety of small arms. But eventually we would have been overwhelmed, resorting to evacuating the combat zone in small units to evade capture. Thankfully it never did come to that. Day after day, we avoided detection, re-emerging in the darkness to march across the desert. We searched for targets to attack, slowly picking off small, isolated units of the 10th Mountain Division. The U.S. Command HQ must have experienced a growing sense of frustration as we remained a shadowy, elusive enemy, our pin prick attacks frustratingly effective in wearing down their massive force. They had a huge hammer, but missed the opportunity to use it on our Airborne mice!

Near the end, I recall one night move in particular. Our platoon was crossing an expanse of desert, quietly flitting from one position of concealment to another in our 3-4 man teams.

"Halt! Enemy in sight!" The whispered warning went up and down our troops. We hit the dirt, ears cocked for any sounds. We soon found out what awaited us ahead. It was what could have been an armoured regiment in full force, tanks, self-propelled artillery and armoured troop carriers. Also, the Yanks had a new toy in this desert game, armed dune buggies! These were carrying 2-3 men, armed with machine guns and rocket launchers. As these vehicles advanced toward us, we buried our faces into the dirt in fear. One column stopped just in front, no doubt using their state-of-the art Infra red night devices to locate us.

Somehow we remained undetected as the dune buggies and recon elements buzzed around us, like a giant lurking predator. Over the next hour or so, our platoon advanced, leopard crawling over the desert sand, inch by inch. As we passed vehicle after vehicle, we listened amazed as the crew's overhead talked over their radio intercoms. They suspected we were in the area, but had no idea where we were exactly! A few brave lads even had the temerity to get up and scrawl insults with chalk on the sides of their armoured vehicles. If we had live IED's and this was real combat, we would have attached them to the prized targets. But being a war game, we were happy to get through that armoured fist undetected. We left the enemy armour behind eventually, unscathed and ignorant of the fact we had just infiltrated their position and disappeared like a ghost into the night.

The next morning, we found a new, juicy target. We spotted and scouted a fairly large force of Americans in the early morning twilight. Over the next few hours, the four platoons of 3 Commando gathered like a snake around the unsuspecting Yanks. We manoeuvered slowly into our attacking positions, using the heavy weapons (mortars and machine guns as our support base. Then para flares arced into the sky and the assault went in. It was like one of Thor's lightning bolts, striking the off guard American force with our characteristic speed and force. It was over in minutes, once more victory was hours. Dozens of vehicles, hundreds of men stood in our midst, staring dumbly at our pointed weapons. It dealt a mortal blow to 10th Mountain Division, as we also captured a unit HQ with several high-ranking officers. Likewise, the other Commandos had achieved similar successes, disrupting and throwing into chaos our enemy.

My platoon mates and I took the occasion to pillage supplies from the Yank's huge stores of rations, water and ammo. Shouts of "10 Platoon was here! 3 Commando rules! Airborne" reverberated in the early dawn desert air. We grinned in triumph as we walked by disgruntled U.S. soldiers, smoking looted cigarettes and drinking from our desert canteens. We must have looked intimidating, our skin camouflaged in black and green, not having shaved or washed in days, loaded for bear with gear and brandishing a variety of weapons. After a brief period of chaotic victory celebrations, the NCO's regained control over their wild, victory imbued paratroopers. "10 Platoon! Fall in, prepare to move out!"

My section leader Ernie Hall stood before us, his slitted eyes showing no emotion as he glared at his younger soldiers. "OK section. Check your weapons, prepare too march! Gill how is your ammo?" I answered that I was getting low, something like 30 rounds for my rifle and a few pyrotechnic explosives. I had maybe a day's rations left but had refilled my two canteens. Physically and emotionally I felt on the top of my game, so could continue for days.

Ex. Border Star was abruptly concluded on March 31, when the U.S. 10th Mountain Division threw in the towel. We heard later from some American officers that they were impressed with our Airborne Regiment. They had failed to capture a single paratrooper, while being outguessed and out manoeuvered over the week of the war game. It could have gone on for another week, but they called it off early feeling a bit humiliated. Shortly after End-Ex, the three Commando companies marched to collection points after receiving orders and compass headings. Soon after our land taxis arrived to transport us back to Fort Bliss. These were U.S. Army 5 ton trucks, the officers and a few lucky men flying back in Huey and

Chinook helicopters. I sat in the rear of a 5 ton, hours of bumpy riding across the desert. When the tail gate lowered, we jumped down, shaking off a coat of fine desert sand.

"Jeez! Where the hell have you fellahs been?" The Yank drivers stared at us laughing, for we must have looked a sight. A solid week spent in the desert wilderness, not having seen showers or any luxuries for days. After returning to Fort Bliss, our immediate duty was to our weapons. We cleaned the filthy barrels and mechanisms after stripping them, using varsol baths to remove baked on dirt and carbon from firing hundreds of rounds of blank cartridges. Our gleaming, clean weapons were inspected before turning them into our Commando stores. The Desert training was over, these weapons and our gear being flown back to Canada in C-130's. At the after-action O-group, I was detailed to join one of the Hercs as security. In a few days, I would fly the long flight to Edmonton, Alberta. As Major Leavy addressed us, I stood in the massed ranks of 3 Commando, with an intense feeling of pride and accomplishment.

He heaped praise on his command, telling us how proud he was each of us. It was a real, challenging test, he barked at us. No one, including the Americans really knew what would happen, as this was a first trial of Airborne against this new, untried Mountain Division. American officers also said a few words, reiterating what our OC had said. Lessons were learned on both sides, ultimately benefitting both units. As future conflicts loomed, primarily in Yugoslavia, Africa and the Middle East, we had learned how the American Army worked and how we could operate in close conjunction with them. Unfortunately, our leaders back home ignored these valuable lessons in the coming decade, throwing it all away. But for now, we celebrated a successful desert operation. For two days, we were given leave to experience the city of El Paso and across the Rio Grande, the Mexican city of Juarez.

A brief word on camouflage uniforms, which every Canadian soldier wears today (2019), from administrative clerks working in our cities to sailors and airmen. In my service and in the desert, we did not wear camouflage uniforms. We wore olive drab combat pants and shirts. When we came out that day in late March 1985, they were not green anymore. We were covered from head to toe in a thick coat of desert dust, oil and layer on layer of camouflage skin cream. We had not shaved, washed or changed clothes in nearly a week. It worked, we blended into the desert like we were part of it. The Americans only saw us when we appeared out of the early morning mist to attack them, like ghosts, then vanished shortly after. So, there was no need to for sexy new cam uniforms. Yes, they would have been nice to change into new uniforms, but good soldiers do not rely on this.

The next morning, The Airborne Regiment was given leave to visit the city of El Paso and the surrounding area, apart from a few unlucky ones who remained on duty, manning Op's and guarding our lines. Ernie Hall my section commander declined, choosing to go snake hunting in the desert. After the buses dropped my platoon off, we headed across the border into Mexico. We walked across a bridge over the Rio Grande into Juarez. It looked more like a dried-up creek to me, as I joked to the lads. "We had a similar creek on our farm when I was a kid. We used to swim in it after a hot day working the fields and tending our cattle. Or we walked down to the Nation River about an acre away to fish from an old row boat. This is a tributary of the Ottawa River, that flows north to the Airborne's base at Petawawa."

That morning we shopped in the stores of Juarez, where I haggled with a Mexican vendor, purchasing my first and only pair of cowboy boots. I also bought a cowboy hat and a few other things, before we hit a few bars. Clint Eastwood would have been proud, as I strutted about trying to resemble my favourite actor. We tasted the local tequila, Mescal, a fiery, brownish drink, with a worm in the bottle. As we walked the streets, we noticed local Mexican street toughs following us. We sensed they were sizing us up for a scrap, probably mistaking us for Yankee gringos. We laughed and taunted them, advising them not to try anything foolish. They disappeared without incident, eventually we returned to El Paso, for a night of festivities.

There was a large group of us assembling for the night, so in Airborne fashion, we located a half descent motel and booked into a few rooms. Some guys were dispatched to buy booze, then we looked for some clubs. I ended up at one big dance club, stunned by the beautiful young women. They were the first I had seen up close in the past month. I danced with one tallish, dark haired beauty, who told me she was half U.S/half Mexican. But alas, she was not buying my Canadian allure, although she said I was attractive. She did earn my respect though, admitting I had a girl friend back home. A few hours later, finished with the bars and getting low on money, we returned to the motel. A major party started then as we broke into the liquor hoard. Then we heard a rumour, one of our new lads by the name of MacDonald had been jumped downtown by Americans. He had been beaten and robbed, ending up in hospital. As we took this in somberly, a few Yanks blundered into our hotel room.

"We just want to party with y'all!" We politely asked them to leave as we were mourning our buddy. As we got steadily drunker, the two annoying guests refused to leave. So, I escorted them outside and told them to take their leave. It ended up in a brief scrap, which finally convinced them they were not welcome. "It's nothing personal. We don't like any legs, including out own in Canada." This was a term we used for anybody not in the Airborne Regiment. It meant "lacking enough guts" to jump from a perfectly serviceable airplane.

The next day, we had a nice breakfast, chatting over the crazy night. Another of our guys had gone missing. It turned out he was arrested by Mexican police and was in jail. He had reported being robbed, lost his wallet and military I.D. I heard it took our ambassador and foreign affairs diplomats to finally spring him free weeks later. Probably for a few dollars under the table. That day went by in a haze, as we resumed partying, trying to empty the bars of their booze stock and as many of the local Mexicali girls as we could carry. I remember returning to our desert base camp late the following morning, with our drunken gang singing filthy songs as we hung from the bus windows. After dumping our gear and changing into our clean clothes, it was off to our drinking mess tent. It was a wild, uproarious affair as we attempted to drink that mess dry as well.

Our C.O. finally ordered the M.P.'s to put an end to our final desert party. It ended up in near mutiny, as we threatened the M.P.'s with nasty things. In the end, we satisfied ourselves, mostly 2 Commando in the lead, by burning some of the wooden benches in our camp fire outside the tent. Then mysteriously the C.O. relented and opened the bar for another hour or so. I heard later it was the R.S.M. Collier who had interceded wisely, thus averting a scene. Then as the booze went dry finally, we staggered back to our tents, sleeping the rest of the night away blissfully. It felt like minutes to me, when I heard the N.C.O.'s bawling at us to get on parade in ten minutes.

I felt my head swimming as I pulled on my boots and donned the maroon beret and staggered out of the tent flap to join the rest of 10 Platoon.

"Duties for the flight back to Canada. Gilligan you will be security on a Herc flying to Edmonton. Any questions? Off you go, the rest of the platoon will fly back to Trenton. Two weeks leave when we dismiss at Pet. Then we fly to Dundern, where the advance party, including you Gill, will rejoin us." So, I embarked onto said Hercules shortly after, along with about a dozen other assigned Airborne as security. I looked sadly back at the desert scene I was leaving behind. It had been a wild, crazy but successful trip I thought. We had done the job and the Yanks, especially 10th Light Mountain Division would not forget us soon! The Load Master waited till we were all aboard, then raised the rear ramp. As the Herc taxied down the runway, I saluted the men I was leaving behind, then sat down on a seat and buckled up.

It took most of the day before we reached Edmonton Airport. It was my first trip back since my Basic Para course in November 1983. The highlight of the trip was when I was invited to the pilot's cabin to view the Earth far below. It must have been around 20,000 feet, I was very impressed with the Herc crew and the overall scene. I even got to crash out in a bunk behind the pilots for a few hours of welcome rest. When I awoke later I was served dinner as I lay on the cot. I stayed in the cabin, observing the flight crew fly the plane north across the border to land at Edmonton. It was a rare chance to see this huge transport land from the cockpit. I almost felt like a normal passenger on an airline! Of course, it was short lived, my idealic ride in heaven. After landing I looked out of the cabin windows to see what? Snow of course! It was in the first week of April I believe as we veteran desert rats reluctantly debarked from the rear ramp, after the C-130 transport lumbered to a stop near a hangar. I felt pretty good, apart from shivering in the chill Arctic blasts, as Alberta embraced my body once more.

AIRBORNE PRAIRIE TRAINING

I had a deep tan going, but was dressed not in Arctic gear, but regular combat fatigues, sleeves rolled up! My skin was going numb quickly as we dashed about unloading pallets of gear and vehicles from several Hercules. After the job was done, guards were posted in a revolving shift in the hangar. It was boring, monotonous duty, not like the hectic field training we had become used to. The next day, the senior NCO in charge sent me on leave for a week. I was overjoyed at this unexpected surprise. The Army and the world loved me then I thought.

    I ended up going to Lake Louise in the Rocky Mountains to do some down hill skiing. I had done quite a bit, as the Ottawa-Montreal area where I grew up had some descent hills for skiing. Also when I was posted to Europe, I experienced real mountains, the Alps of Bavaria and Switzerland. Lake Louise is of course serious downhill skiing being in the Rockies. It was also potentially life threatening, many a novice or experienced skier or hiker meeting their end over the years. Unperturbed I entered the mouth of the shark, skiing from lodge to lodge. I finished each day satiated, exhausting my adrenaline supplies, booked into my luxurious hotel room to get cleaned up. Then I hit the town to see what kind of trouble I could stir up. But I had a good time over that week, wisely staying under the radar, so to speak. Then again with some reluctance, it was time to report back for duty in Edmonton. I arrived at C.F.B. Namao after leave, where our regimental and commando stores had been moved from Edmonton's International Airport. We were briefed that the following week, we would drive the vehicles and stores in a convoy to Dundern Saskatchewan.

M/Cpl Hebert was my NCO at this time, replacing Hall. From 1-23 April, I was part of RV 85 Advance party for the Airborne Regiment. "What the hell is Dundern?" Voices blurted out as the NCO smiled at us. Dundern is a small town, about 40 km. south of Saskatoon, several hundred kilometers north-east of C.F.B. Edmonton. We had an easy time guarding our gear in Edmonton, being as it was at a secure military base. I even got the chance to pop in at the Airborne Training Center, located in North

Edmonton at Greisbach Military Base.[6] There I watched in some satisfaction as the latest baby paratroopers went through the gruelling ground training before jump week. It was surreal I thought, joking with the Airborne instructors. "That was 17 months ago or so, yet it feels like it was yesterday." They nodded saying this was common, adding they had heard we had performed well in Texas. "Keep it up Trooper. So, boot camp in Dundern eh? Then on to RV 85." Dundern I heard was our warm up "battle school" to prep us for RV 85, the biggest exercise of the year in Canada. It was scheduled to last from 23rd April to 18th of May, we would be in Dundern for about a month before RV 85 began.

"Ah a piece of cake buddy! After winter warfare, desert warfare, mountains, ect. Is there nothing intimidating for Airborne paratroopers?' During this time, a break in the action so to speak, I had time to reflect on my military career to date. I had passed my first decade in the Canadian Forces, all as an infantrier, a grunt as the American term labels it. The first eight years I spent in the Reserves with the Cameron Highlanders of Ottawa, achieving the rank of Sergeant. The last three were as a member of the RCR and Airborne Regiment. After making the switch I was given the rank of TQ 3 Private, then

---

6 In a weird twist of fate, I would end up buying my first property across from Greisbach, some twenty years later. This base had then been decommissioned, after the Canadian Airborne was disbanded by the Liberal Gov't. in 1994.

transferred to 3 Commando in the summer of 1983. I spent the next three years passing one qualification after another, so in 1985 I reached the highest level of my rank, TQ 5 I was a super qualified grunt. As the days dragged by in Edmonton, I came off the high of the U.S. deployment. I was now a qualified desert soldier, Winter warfare expert, paratrooper with 31 jumps, mountain warfare, machine gunner, anti-tank expert and trained NCO. My last job before going direct entry into the Regular Force was an instructor on a Pre-Reserve Officer Course in Camp Borden, Ontario.

    I was getting a bit frustrated however, for my promotion to Corporal was proceeding slowly. Part of this was because I was in the Airborne Regiment. I was told promotions were slow and few and far between. Also, there was a high level of competition, for I was up against the best soldiers in the Army. So, there was pressure to get back to the RCR, where my promotion was virtually guaranteed. When I did, I was surprised to learn my direct superior, with the rank of Master Corporal had never been deployed to a field exercise or overseas. His only course was the Level 6, for promotion to M/Cpl. It was a travesty for me, I had vastly more experience, yet was a mere private! Finally, the advance party and security detachment were given the word to travel to Dundern. It was a relief, for the more I sat waiting, the more time I had to think about the unfairness of life. We were paired off in the vehicles, then sent packing.

Late that afternoon, we arrived at Dundern at last. We parked the vehicles and reported in to the base orderly office. We unloaded our personal gear and assigned to barracks, awaiting the arrival of the whole Airborne Regiment the following day. Off duty for the evening, a dozen or so of the advance party went to the nearby Dundern hotel. A few hours later it started, an event so trivial but important, it would affect me for quite a while. I was sitting at a table reflecting on my life, when a ruckus began at the pool table nearby. I walked over and asked what it was about. By now there were two of us left from the advance party. The rest of the hotel customers were civilians. One of them informed me that my buddy from E Battery had tried to pick up an Indian woman, so they would teach him his manners. I saw this soldier was being pinned by two of the civilians, before they planned to drag him outside for a beating.

"That's not happening. He is my buddy, if you want to scrap, you'll have to face me as well." They accepted this enthusiastically, as they outnumbered us by about 12:1. So outside we went, then the civilians jumped us. My buddy who was not very big had minimal input as two of the attackers pinned him to a wall and began punching him. Personally, I vaguely remember what happened over the next few minutes, being assailed on all sides. It was a fight for survival, but I was dishing out punishment to those who wanted to strike me. Luckily Sly Sylvester has trained me in martial arts, which proved to be very helpful. Then the biggest man came at me, rushing in with great enthusiasm. I sidestepped his punch, flipping him over my back, then ending it with a hard judo kick. I saw him topple head over ass down a stairwell, yelling for dear life! Shortly after the fight ended, as the local RCMP arrived. The civilians had changed their tune by now, releasing my fellow Airborne buddy, accusing us of instigating the whole affair. The RCMP put us in the back of the cruiser, driving to Dundurn's MP shack for questioning. We were told to give a statement, then we would be released.

As I sat waiting, before me were some of the civilians who had been engaged with us. I recall as the fight progressed their numbers had steadily increased, which I stated in my statement as approaching twenty. I caught the eye of the big man, who had cuts and bruises over his face. I remarked casually, "Think you had it tough? You picked on two of us tonight. Tomorrow hundreds of my brother Airborne lads will arrive. When they hear what you did, I feel sorry for you and this town." I was venting a bit, but the effect I found later was mercurial. The crap hit the fan the next morning, as the Airborne Regiment arrived in full force. We received a briefing, making Dundern town out of bounds for the duration of our stay. Apparently, they were terrified of revenge, possibly the complete destruction of the town and burning of the hotel where we were attacked. Then Major Leavy called me in for an immediate interview.

I suspected I was in some trouble, so I calmly related what had happened. I felt I was doing my duty, in backing up my fellow Airborne brother. The major did not look pleased, but when I responded I had won the fight, he relaxed a bit. I was stunned when he told me the RCMP were considering charging me with assault and battery, based on the witness accounts of numerous civilians from the Dundern hotel. The OC said he would back me up as far as he could. In fact, he saved my hide, for the RCMP dropped the charges and things calmed down. Major Leavy talked to me after, saying they had come to an agreement. He had considered my good reputation so far in 3 Commando, saying if I was not a good soldier, I would have ended up in prison for several months. Then probably at the whim of the Regimental C.O. be dishonourably discharged from the Forces. It was a near miss, a reminder on how fast the world could turn on one at any time. After I was dismissed, I returned to my brothers in 10 Platoon.

Soon after summer boot camp began, starting off with daily runs and rucksack marches to drill us into shape once more. I was assigned to carry the Karl Gustav 84 mm rocket launcher, one of the heaviest, bulkiest weapons one could carry. But I did not care, happy to be back with my Para mates. Also, it was one of my strongest specialties, Anti-tank weapons. I fired live, about three rounds on April 30 of that month, hitting the target repeatedly. A big task was digging trenches, establishing a replica of a Russian company defensive position. Then we attacked it using various means. I was paired with another platoon mate, using live fire we jumped into the trench, firing live rounds at dummy targets. Then we threw live grenades into the underground bunkers and destroyed any dummy targets. I entered the final bunker, filled with smoke from the M-67 grenade thrown by Higgins. I had fixed my bayonet to the end of my FN C1 rifle before going in. Crouching in the dark bunker I saw a Figure 11 target in one corner. I fired immediately, putting two 7.62 rounds into the figure's face, then lunged forward and buried my bayonet into the stomach. I followed this by kicking it, smashing it into the ground. We emerged to a crowd of onlookers, high ranking officers there to observe. They watched as we crawled out of the trench, face blackened by cordite and dirt. I was happy for this was by now my natural element. "War what the hell is it good for?", to quote Bruce Springsteen.

Also part of the Airborne Battle school was re-qualifying on every weapon in the Airborne arsenal, apart from the 105mm howitzers belonging to E Battery 2 RCHA. We practiced our techniques of unarmed combat, taking out sentries, night patrolling and navigation and countless cross country hikes. During our off time, we formed a new rugby team, playing our first challenge match against the local Saskatoon team. They beat us in a close match, then invited us to their local club, a bar in Saskatoon termed The Artful Dodger. It turned out to be an eye opener, leading to a permanent Airborne rugby team. I loved it so much, I continued playing for various civilian teams for the next fifteen years. It nearly matched my love of parachuting and firing weapons (eventually becoming a trained sniper).

That night was a special one, for I also met a new girl friend. A group of women arrived and sat at a table near my rugby squad. Our officer, a young greenie, had the first go at them. After being rejected by the laughing women, I volunteered to be next. Asking if I could sit down and join them, one smiling girl waved me in. I smiled at my mates nearby, then sat beside the lovely young lady. I introduced myself first, then found out they were celebrating one of their sister's upcoming wedding. I nodded and added my congratulations, adding I would buy a round for them. I talked with Gloria beside me, explaining my unit 3 Commando of the Airborne were in the area training for the next month, before parachuting into Wainwright, Alberta. We hit it off that night, for they invited (just me) to join them in bar-hopping through Saskatoon city. Much later as we staggered singing into a final bar, well into the early morning, these lovely ladies actually saved me. A bunch of cowboys, who knew these ladies, did not like my presence, threatening to do something nasty to me. The oldest sister who I love to this day, spoke up. "Sonny lay one hand on our friend here, and it will be the last time you ever get laid in this city!" I laughed uproariously as the cowboys backed off, with their tails between their legs.

After more drinks in this bar, I wound up at their house. I retired to bed finally, led by the lovely youngest sister Gloria. Finally, as the morning approached I said I had to get to base for morning parade. These women packed me into a taxi, giving the driver several bills.

The first thing I saw getting out of said taxi, was God himself. Or to me he was, my Sergeant Major back at Dundern base. I staggered before him, attempting a parody of a salute. He gave me a stiff glare, informing me to be on parade in ten minutes, dressed for a run-in PT gear. I thanked him as I staggered off, reminding myself of the error. He was not an officer but the senior most NCO in the Regiment, therefore not to be saluted. Ten minutes later I ran out in PT gear, then commenced a five miler at a descent pace, dreaming of that lovely maiden.

The platoon NCO setting the pace was in a hurry I quipped as we took off at a fast clip. It did the job though, getting rid of the last lingering effects of my night out. The prairie countryside flew by, finally we returned to camp some 35 minutes later. It showed 10 Platoon was in top gear, no one having fallen out. Just the usual people puking their guts out. As we stretched after, I was quizzed on my idealic night in Saskatoon. I said I had been keeping up the Airborne's image with the civilian population, suggesting I should get the job of public relations. Indeed it set the standard for the rest of the month. Every spare moment I had, following my rugby team's odd game, was spent with my new girl friend. Gloria was very nice, having just broken off with her boyfriend recently. So, I was happy to fill the void, not mentioning I had another girl friend back in Ottawa. But my platoon mates knowing this, had endless joy in reminding me that I was a cheat. "No names no pack drill! Besides I need cheering up after my first rude greeting here!"

The next big thing was following our last rugby match with Saskatoon's team. It was a fun game, not really counting for much. Slowly 3 Commando's team was learning the game, as for most of us it was new. I had played football in high school as a linebacker on defense. The final year I was named a team captain, my first go as a leader. After this, I attended Carleton University, playing several years for the Carleton Ravens football squad. For my initiation, we rookies had to stand on a table naked and swill a jug of beer, as the veterans taunted us and sprayed beer over us. We also worked in the Alumni pub as bouncers on big nights. Frequently we had to eject problem drunkards. It was good practice for the Army, as I found fighting was a way of life. One memorable night, a group of bikers crashed the pub festivities. As they were not students, with no I.D., the head bouncer decided they had to go. They were not cooperative in this, so we forcibly convinced them to leave. One leather clad biker left through a plate glass window, as I assisted another bouncer in heaving him out.

After the rugby match, it was off to the Artful Dodger Pub for the standard beer and wings. By now the owner knew us well, as did Gloria and her sisters. A band was on stage that evening, as we enjoyed the hospitality. Then a local bike gang arrived, changing the mood immediately. I listened as a biker ordered the owner to get rid of the band. He replied if they did not like the music, they could leave. The biker then flattened him, punching the older man senseless. I did not hesitate, setting my beer glass down, I stepped up to the grinning biker, standing over the prone owner. "Hey buddy, try someone your own size." Then the fight erupted, as I exchanged blows with the biker. It ended quickly, five minutes later or so, as I stood over the knocked out biker. I looked up to see bodies lying on the floor all around.

The fight was handled solely by my Airborne rugby team, several of whom were accomplished black belts, including my good friend Sylvester. The civvy rugby team barely had time to get on their feet before it was over. One of them, who was a Saskatoon police officer alerted the quick reaction squad, who arrived soon after. We helped the owner to his feet, who told the police that the instigators were the bikers, who lay groaning on the floor. As they were arrested and carted off, the police were told to leave us alone. The grateful owner, rewarded us with free rounds for the rest of the evening. I assured the owner that we would protect the bar from any further biker actions, knowing they would want revenge. Then I returned to my table, where Gloria and her friends looked at us like their saviours. It was a surreal, successful evening, as I left with Gloria, escorting her safely back to her sister's house. Again they invited me to stay, regaling them with heroic deeds as they treated me to a late-night snack and liquor. As it turned out, the feared biker revenge never materialized, so apparently they learned their lesson. Gloria eventually dragged me off to her bedroom, soon taking my mind off the night's frantic business. Hours later, this gorgeous young lady drove me back to Dundurn, kissing me good-bye. The only bad thing was, I did not get much rest. Shortly afterward, I joined 10 Platoon in another long march in full combat gear across the Prairie training area.

Our platoon officer, 2nd Lieutenant Patchet led the way, carrying his pea shooter, a pistol. I carried the Karl Gustav rocket launcher and about sixty pounds of combat gear. So I sweated blood during that march, my youthful exuberance and experience getting me through the day. We did not return to base, marching out to the live fire ranges. All day we fired hundreds of rounds, zeroing our personal weapons and taking care of any issues. Soon we knew, our idealic time in Saskatoon was about to end. RV 85 was looming, starting with a mass drop into Wainwright army base. On May 11, we warmed up with a parachute drop into a makeshift DZ on Dundurn base. It was my 32nd military static line jump, out of a CH 147 Chinook, the medium lift chopper, with dual rotor blades, and most importantly a rear ramp. I flied into the chopper in the #4 port stick for the drop onto DZ

Hammer. This became my favourite jump, a bonus being we had no equipment. It was an administrative "bare ass" drop, usual reserved for foreign guests or senior ranks, because it was so easy. It took me over two years in the Borne to finally get a jump out of one, although I had ridden in them many times.

We jumped one stick at a time, filing up to the rear ramp, staring down at the panoramic scene of the Dundurn DZ a thousand feet below the Huey. I rocked on my feet, holding the static line as the big chopper rocked back and forth as the pilot levelled out. Given the go ahead, he flicked the light from red to green. The first jumper hurled off the ramp, as the stick started forward at a slow jog. I saw the chutes billow open before I jumped off the ramp.

It was quite different from going out the side door of a Herc, no nasty prop blast to greet one. There was a perfect view of the proceedings, as I looked down at the ground below. Then a gentle tug, as the main chute billowed open over my helmet. As I came in to land a half minute later, I saw an old shell crater. Too late to avoid it, I braced for the landing. Also, I was blown backwards by the wind, which was rare. I ended up cart wheeling backwards, sustaining a sore neck and a slight ankle sprain. "Damn it!" I cursed under my breath as I got up, brushing sand off my uniform. I was checked out by a medic, but cleared of any serious injuries. 10 Platoon then had to route march back to base, on the orders of our eager young officer, eager to impress the boss, Major Leavy. After my ankle started to get really sore, Platoon Warrant Officer Palmer asked the officer to slow the pace a bit. Carrying his 9 mm SMG he snorted, telling us to suck it up. As we sweated the miles away, the grumbling started.

Finally we reached a small bridge over a prairie stream, just before getting to the main base. Warrant Palmer said he thought the young officer needed a bath. Just as we stepped onto the bridge, the trap was sprung, two soldiers grabbing the officer and dragging him down the slope to the river. Just before they were about to douse him in the water, he managed to slip away. Setting the Karl G rocket launcher down I arrived to the rescue. We shouted in joy, as the officer was dragged down the slope, his screams of terror echoing in the air. Then in he went, my hands pinning his arms as he struggled futilely. Just to make sure he got a nice taste of the cool water, I rammed his head below the surface. As I crawled back up the slope to my grinning comrades, Patchet's head emerged from the water. He spat water furiously, not at all amused.

"Who was that? Warrant take his name!" Palmer gave us the sign to keep quiet. "Sorry Sir, I lost him in the crowd. Time to get back Sir! Platoon quick march! Double time!" The flustered young 2nd Lieutenant fell in the rear as the platoon, re-energized now sprinted the rest of the way onto the base, our laughing and shouts of 10 Platoon echoing off the barracks buildings, many onlookers staring at us amused. I was picked up later by Gloria, for another joyful night in the city. I told her later of the day's activities, laughing my self silly.

"OMG! It was crazy. Theoretically it was assault on a senior officer! If the CO would have got my name, I could be in jail right now!" Gloria smiled, leaning into my arm, never had she felt as good as she did that night. It was like being in heaven, all the weight of the Airborne lifted from my shoulders. After exchanging a kiss, I whispered in her ear that I loved her. Indeed, if she asked, I would have proposed to her right there. Damn the world and all, but it was a special moment. It continued to grow over that final week, until finally 3 Commando were given the word. May 19 would be our last day in Saskatchewan, for the RV 85 Op. had arrived. I called Gloria that last day, listening to her sad good-bye. I would never see or hear from her again.

RV 85: That day the Airborne Regiment was trucked to our airhead, located at Saskatoon's main airport. In our briefings, we were told the DZ was at Seville Farm, located in the isolated netherlands of the sprawling Wainwright base. Ominously the place where I was to land was called Rifle Ridge. It was a TEN, tactical, full equipment night jump. A mass drop, the entire regiment loaded into about 24 Hercules C-130's. This was practically the entire Air Force's fleet of these big transports. Dropped in the dead of night, or early morning as it turned out. Outside of war, it was the hardest drop to make. Loaded with maximum weight till one could barely stand, especially the machine gunners and the Karl G rocket launchers. I was told I was manifested as #2 Port side, pleased to be near the front of the line. Then after getting dressed, we waited for Zero hour, my thoughts on Gloria, leaving behind the bliss of Saskatoon. I did not know then what would happen, but I love her to this day.

Mission: The Canadian AB Regiment will embark C-130's in Saskatoon and parachute into DZ Saville Farm to engage enemy forces during RV 85 from May 19 to 29 June 1985.

It was part of a two and a half months of intensive training for the Borne. Trains went west from Ontario on April 14, followed by Boeing and chartered aircraft on April 19 with the bulk of the Regiment. It was the decision and efforts of the Commander, Colonel Ian Douglas and his side kick Major Gene Markel, the Regimental Major to use Dundurn as the base for boot camp. During that time, it was the only Regular Army tenant at the camp. The rest of the Army were crammed into Camp Wainwright's training area. This is where my Advance Party rejoined our specific units for training. The Commandos kicked off with range work, conducting zeroing, grouping and rapid fire applications on ranges constructed by the paratroopers. These temporary ranges were superb, thanks to the initiative and expertise of the NCOs. The one constructed by Sergeant Connick of the Armoured

Defence Platoon was so well cleared and constructed it grabbed praise from the senior officers. After shooting week, the usual competitions began, with 2 CDO winning the SMG and FN C2, with 3 CDO getting the gold on the FNC1 rifle. 1 CDO dominated on Sports Day near the end.

Then on May 18 Exercise Bear Claw, a Regimental exercise began. The mission orders were to seize a bridgehead line along the Battle River. NLT 20 0800 hrs. May 18, 1985. The Commandos were to jump in the general vicinity of Seville Farm, the DZ held and marked by the Pathfinder Platoon. In the event, the bridgehead was captured a day early on May 19th, the enemy force played by ADP and machine gun platoons. 1 and 3 Commandos used air mobile operations to out-manoeuvre the enemy, then linked up with 2 Commando who marched on foot. Then after a day to clean up and re-organize, the Regiment took on the rest of the SSF Brigade FTX, fighting a delaying withdrawal back to the Battle River. 1 Commando fought a separate battle, winning at the Karki and Blue bluffs, while 3 Commando used a box ambush with superb results against the SSF enemy. 2 Commando destroyed a couple of Tactical Headquarters, this accomplishment remaining a secret under the orders of the SSF Commander BGen Corbould.

HQ and Sigs finished the enemy off just before End Ex. The Commandos thanked their OC Major Prior and his small band of warriors for the unexpected break to reorganize and rest.

The last part was Exercise Proud Warrior, the big Divisional Exercise. The Pathfinders were again first in, one day before the main body, practicing their Escape & Evasion against the enemy force played by 5 Svc. Bn. Then we dropped on Rifle Ridge, without a hitch, mostly. This is where I was injured severely, the worst of my career so far. 3 Commando moved quickly to seize Cataloo Bridge, mainly led by my 10 Platoon...minus myself. At this point early that night, I had landed on Rifle Ridge, ironically the barrel of my FNC1 rifle penetrated my left leg. A medic Randy Corcoran got to me a half hour later and began administering first aid, as I was bleeding slowly to death. It was pitch black as several guys stumbled about me, one stepping on the rifle jammed inside my left thigh. I cursed and told Crawford to pick up his feet, but it was a mess, with the chute, lines and equipment all tangled up. After clearing the gear away, Cochoran removed the barrel of the rifle from my leg, bandaged and splinted my leg.

I found out later of 3 Commando successful seizure of the bridge, the startled enemy unable to hold their positions as the rest of the regiment crossed the creek, dry for the first time ever. The battle for the bridge raged on relentlessly, but with Service Commando in depth, held on until relieved by follow up divisional units. This took the boring, mundane task of defending from the aggressively trained paratroopers. This gave the Airborne the chance to go on the offensive, for the next day area interdictions, the bread and butter of the Airborne occurred. The war stories I heard later were rivalled only by the new Sylvester Stalone movie RAMBO. The Ex ended with a few live fire assaults, then the redeployment back to Petawawa occurred in the last week of June. It was a long haul, but a superb opportunity to soldier in the shop window of the 3rd Division, putting in a 100 % effort, proving the Airborne was trained to a razor edge. Unfortunately, I missed the last part due to the severity of my injury. I was medivacked from Rifle Ridge in the rear of an ambulance. It was a long, bumpy ride to the Field Hospital as I had landed in a road-less piece of back country. Then I was stripped of my gear and lay naked on a metal gurney for over an hour as we waited for a civilian doctor to arrive from Edmonton. I had not been given any pain killer or morphine yet, so the pain was starting to rear its ugly head. But I talked to the nurses to take my mind off it.

I never yelled or screamed, even after I saw the severity of the damage, my thigh being torn open. It occurred to me I could die if things went bad, or lose my leg if infection set in. As it turned out, after talking to the civilian surgeon, I relaxed a bit. He seemed confident and at ease, even joking with me, assuring he would give his best effort. Then I was put under, awaking the next morning in a cot in the field hospital tent. The medics and nurses assured me my legs were still attached, then they served me breakfast. I joked that if I was not hurt, I would be eating out of a hole in the ground, in the middle of nowhere! Indeed I let them know, that my first thoughts immediately after the landing, while the medic worked on my leg, were to Warrant Pryce, "Patch me up and get me back to the platoon Sir.' It was a tedious grind for the next two weeks, the main worry was clean and changing bandages daily to prevent infection. By the second week though, the doctor said he was pleased that the surgery had gone well and there were no complications.

I managed to get out of bed and begin exercising near that second week. I also was visited by a few members of my platoon, which cheered me up immensely. One of my buddies Rick Dorion told me he had the task of cleaning my rifle. He said it stank, the barrel had pieces of my leg stuck to it, also it was covered in muck and rust due to the rain that evening. Then they wished me luck and headed off, leaving me to get on with my rehab exercises. Later the press arrived, talking to the patients and taking some photos. Later my parents sent me one photo, which showed me recovering in my cot, printed in The Ottawa Citizen News.

After being cleared to travel, I was shipped back to Petawawa on a C-130, strapped to a pallet by Sergeant Rockheim, one of my Airborne Depot Instructors. He assured me it was a rule, just in case there was an aircraft emergency in the air. I laughed and slept most of the long six-hour flight. When I was carried off the plane finally, it was the first time back since early March. A four-month non-stop deployment, but this was soon to be eclipsed. It was in August, 3 Commando emplaned for the Mediterranean Island of Cyprus, separated from the Airborne Regiment, as well as our home in Petawawa for the next seven months. It seemed like much longer, for we were under the orders of 2 RCHA, who hated the Airborne as we would soon discover. In the last week of June, while in the Petawawa base hospital, the doctor gave me some medical leave for a week or so. My father picked me up after I phoned home. I still had to be checked daily at a hospital for safety protocols, but it was a relief to finally be out of hospital. I returned to duty in July, just in time for the Regimental Change of Command. Colonel Bucky Douglas was handing over the reigns to the new guy, Colonel J.M. Gaudreau. Immediately he let it be known his approach would be tough. He would fire any trooper who became an administrative or disciplinary problem. Maximum time was to be spent in training, for that elusive war in the future. It was to be a recurring theme in the rest of my military career, hard training, discipline and no enemy in sight.

After over a month since my injury, I was returned to full duty in the Airborne. On July 4, I exited a C-130 over DZ Anzio, my slot being #16 port stick. It was my glorious return to this DZ, the last being in February. It was also my first since being' injured in Wainwright. It was an easy, administrative jump though, daylight with no equipment, as it was for the CO Change of Command. Jump #34 went off without a hitch, then we gathered at the DZ shack. We stood formed up in our Commando companies, watching as the two Commanders parachuted in alone from their personal C-130. Colonel Gaudreau then inspected us for the first time, Colonel Bucky the outgoing CO marching beside him. The following day July 5, we followed this up with the 3 Commando Change of Command, with another jump on DZ Anzio. It was basically the same type of jump, wearing our camouflage SSF jump smocks. The only change was I was #18 Starboard side, near the rear of the stick. It took three C-130 planes to get 3 Commando in the air over the drop zone.

Sadly, Major Bill Leavy was relieved by Major Ed Ring. The Bear had been my CO since my first day at 3 Commando and we had seen allot of water go under the bridge, so to speak. After the festivities were over, it was time to gear up for our U.N. posting to Cyprus in August. We received special United Nations training for the next month, receiving ID, drivers permit and a series of needles for diseases and complete medicals.

In July, I had my first vehicle accident, my Dodge Coronet wrecked, after it rolled off the road three times. It was on a Petawawa secondary gravel road and I was going too fast. It was a bitter lesson, knocked out, I found a doctor was stitching my left temple in hospital some time later. I saw my Coronet the next day at an auto shop in the village of Petawawa. It still ran, but the owner advised it would be too costly to repair, thus I sold it for scrap. Shortly after, I bought my second car, a 1980 Ford Mustang.

U.N. DUTY

In the meantime, I was taken off the Cyprus posting, to fight a traffic ticket issued by the base Military Police. I was given a cushy job working on the ranges, jumping once more on DZ Anzio in August. I was starting to like this duty, all jumps were easy administrative jumps. Range work could be monotonous, but being used to it, it did not bother me. In fact, military duty often went from long periods of boredom to intense, hectic periods, then back again. Then one of the new platoon guys got into a fight with some bikers over in Quebec. He was subsequently charged with murder then taken off the Cyprus tour pending the court case. Months later he was found not guilty, as it was self defense.

In the meantime however, I was put back on the Cyprus tour, leaving for the long flight to the island in August. I would not return until the following year in February. It was also I found, the final note on allot of my present life, relationships and my home in The Airborne Regiment. But that was in the future, foggy horizon. Nothing lasts forever I knew, except death and taxes! 3 Commando led by Major Ring boarded the Boeing 707 that day in early September, wearing our new blue berets. We had little idea of what U.N. duty would entail, being new to most of us. We had to learn to curtail our natural, aggressive approach to our duties, becoming in effect policemen to this disputed island between the Greeks and the Turks. It was my second trans-Atlantic flight, the first being in 1979 during posting to 3 RCR based at Baden-Soellingen, West Germany.

Our flight did a stop over in West Germany, landing at CFE Lahr, G.D.R. It was a brief stop, we had a quick chance to see the base before boarding a second plane for the second, long leg to the Mediterranean Sea and Cyprus. We touched down finally at Lanarca Airport, located on the southern shore. 3 Commando then boarded buses for the last leg of the two-day journey, arriving at the capital of Nicosia sometime early in the morning of September 9th. We were briefed we would be stationed in the 'green line" buffer zone, stretching through the old city in a south-easterly direction to the Omorphita Plains. The end of our Sector 4 ended a mile out into the plains, intersecting with Sector 5 where the Swedish contingent took over. This was known as Line East, supposedly the most sensitive part of the entire U.N. demarcation line. 2 RCHA the other part of the contingent ran Line West.

This was strange I thought, as the Artillery Battalion was much larger than 3 Commando, a company sized unit. We had the toughest job with an understrength infantry company, for six months we had to make do. Lightly armed with a rifle and one magazine of twenty rounds. No air support or heavy weapons or reinforcements if the shit did hit the fan, which happened in the 1974 invasion of the island by the Turks. The Airborne Regiment were there in full force then, losing a few paratroopers.

Finally my bus arrived at Ledra Palace, Nicosia. This was a former hotel used by tourists before the last war. Now it was used to house U.N. soldiers when not in the forward lines. From there 10 Platoon grabbed our weapons and gear and arrived at our particular base called Freezenburg House, located in the old city. I was posted on my first 12-hour sentry shift around midnight. It was uneventful, returning to the house after lunch the next day. I met the new platoon Warrant officer, who had just been posted to 3 Commando. We discovered the platoon we had relieved was The Vandoos (R22nd Regiment). It was a large but heavily damaged building, which our platoon had to repair during our off-duty hours over the first month.

Soon after arriving on the island, we were read the riot act by Major Ring. Apparently the Vandoos had a great time on their tour, going wild and wrecking many bars and the platoon houses. So many bars were put out of bounds to 3 Commando to correct the situation. We found the Brit contingent who ran the U.N. force did not like Canadians. Like in the Great World Wars, we colonials were given every dirty job on the island, then blamed if anything went wrong. I wish I could have gotten off that island early, but alas it was not to be.

This would be my final year in the Airborne, posted out the following July to the RCR, I had to bear it and grin. For the first month in September was non-stop activity, with minimum rest periods. Days melded into weeks, weeks into months, a real grind it was. The good thing is our pay increased, with special UN pay, added to our jump pay and basic pay. In October, our platoon was finally taken off line and based in Ledra Palace. Also around that time I mistakenly ended up in one of the out of bounds bars, mentioned previously. Our Canadian M.P.'s put in a report, naming a few of us from 3 Commando and RCHA. The fact is most soldiers did not treat the order seriously, it was more of a recommendation. As not much fazed us, we loved to go into those places few cared to go. So while the officers sorted out the paperwork, on October 8 our platoon was training on Dhekelia, a British base. It was fun, adventure training week, given the choice of scuba diving or freefall parachuting. A few of us chose freefall, joining the local British Freefall Club at Paphos, on the west coast of the island. I did my first basic freefall course, then went skydiving.

On October 6th, I boarded a Cessna 206 single engine aircraft for the first time. There were six of us Airborne, now student skydivers. It was a bright sunny day as we sat on the floor, the pilot climbing to 2200 feet for the jump. We had AeroCom GQ 6.5m rigs with a big round chute. Also being trainees, this was a static line jump, the line hooked to the floor. So it was not a freefall jump... yet. When the door opened, I waited for my turn. There was one Brit instructor who sat by the door and waved us out. We were told to climb out by grabbing the wing and balancing on the landing strut, before launching out into the sky. As I fell, the static line pulled out the main chute, which cracked open over my head. It was a rush of adrenaline, picking up my spirits immensely. I landed OK by the DZ shack, after a lovely view of the island descending the 2000 feet in a few minutes of ecstasy. I did not know it then, but it was the beginning of a whole new life, lasting over decades. I still skydive today, in 2019 (34 years later). The only thing that is still the same is the adrenaline rush The DZ rules, parachutes, equipment, civvy jumpers, the aircraft and myself included, have changed dramatically!

    I only did one jump that day, but it set off a fire in me. Having done over 30 jumps from military aircraft, this first step toward freefall was exciting. I would end up doing five more over the next six months of my tour in Cyprus. The last was on February 9th, 1986 at Kingsfield Airport, at the same height, same aircraft, same rig. I practiced a dummy pull, still being hooked to a static line. The instructor who had a D license remarked in my jump log book "Good. Freefall next!" The things I was learning then were a good, strong exit, body position and arch. That meant getting stable, head up and looking at plane, learning to fly like a bird. But after this, it was back to the army and reality. I did not return to the skydiving world until late 1987, by that time I was no longer an Airborne paratrooper. In July of that year, while attached to 1st Battalion RCR, I got an Honourable Release from the CAF, after twelve years of service.

October 14th: It was back on Line duty, this time at Ortona House, two miles from the Omorphita Plain. It was during this period that I experienced a close call. One night while on a late-night patrol to the Plain to observe any infractions by the opposing Greek Cypriots and the Turkish Army, I walked along the dark road with another soldier. We were told to watch out for booby traps and mines, as this had been an active war zone. Tensions were still high, the two sides separated by mere meters at the narrowest point. As we crept along in silence, suddenly a shot cracked out from my right. I hit the ground instantly, hearing the whizz of the bullet near my ear. "Shit! Call the base! Contact, advise action." I yelled at the other trooper who had the radio set. As I scrambled into cover, I loaded the magazine with twenty of the 7.62 mm ball rounds. However, we were told not to return fire, awaiting the arrival of the duty officer.

We followed orders, not returning fire as more shots whizzed over our heads. It was frustrating being helpless in that kill zone, wearing our blue steel helmets. All our training up to that point was useless now. Except for our common sense, keeping low in whatever cover we could find. Do not panic and stay cool, awaiting the officer to resolve the situation. I joked later it was my first taste of real action, the action I had craved. I felt no fear, but thoughts screamed through my head. I wanted to return fire, but I did not have an exact location, therefore would have wasted my limited supply of ammunition. As it turned out, the guy(s) who had fired on us where from the Greek Cypriot army. It reinforced my impression that they were the poorest trained, ill disciplined lot on the entire island. The officer who interviewed them told us later that these Greek-Cypriot soldiers claimed they had fired at a stray dog or an animal. What a stupid bloody joke I thought. I could have died that night, except these clowns were such poor shots. It was frustrating and angered me later, wishing I would have been given more latitude in engaging this threat, but that is the U.N. Rules are rules...C'est la guerre!

Shortly after this incident, I was rewarded with my first leave pass, two days of freedom from the hectic demands on the green line. With a few mates, we secured a taxi, driving south from Nicosia to Nissi Beach. Spending the day at this topless beach, we mingled with the European women, forgetting the army and its demands. We did some cliff diving, enjoying the hot Med. Sun and swimming to exhaustion. I did not encounter any sharks, but I did see a huge sea snake up close. I thought, "time to go" bolting for the surface. Later that evening, we travelled to the nearby town of Ayanapa. Cyprus, The Island of Venus, as it was known in ancient times, is full of history and archeological ruins. It also has a great nightlife, if one knows where to go. After securing a hotel room, we hit the town to sample the delights of Venus. We ended up at The Cave, a rock bar, relaxing to the music and chatting with the girls. I met a Scottish lass from Glasgow, spending hours dancing and talking about her life back in the Scottish Highlands. It was a fun night, relaxing and helping me to get over the hectic two months on the line. Rudi Rudolf, one of the new replacements that summer, joined me the next night as we returned to the same bar. By chance I met a young Swedish girl, spending most of the night and the next morning with her. I have lasting memories of her big blue eyes staring at me up close, sending tingling sensations up my spine. Then before we knew it, the leave was almost over, back to the grind at Ortona House in Nicosia.

It was a busy time for 3 Commando in the green line. For weeks, I averaged 18 hour days, with 12-hour sentry shifts and more duties after. The women I had met and spent time with that first leave I credit with helping me to cope and get through that time. I was weary most of the time, but never broke. It was just another challenge, an obstacle to overcome. Finally, by November 29th, things eased up a bit. My platoon was tight and performing well I thought. The new Platoon Warrant Hutchins was a prick. There was no love lost between us, but after this stage, even he had grudging respect for me. Allot of Canadian servicemen and women had an easy tour in Cyprus. I did not, but I viewed it as a challenge to be met. I even had thoughts of suicide, something not uncommon there. I got letters from home occasionally, which helped with morale, focussing on finishing this tour and seeing home again. But I was in a somber mood leading up to the holiday season. I worked Christmas Eve, relaxing over the next few days running and working out.

At the end of December, 10 platoon was off line, doing specialized platoon training. One day we put on a show for the Turks and Greeks, on a live fire range. We split into teams and showed off our fire and movement tactics. They seemed impressed as they watched us sprinting forward, then taking cover opening up with our weapons and shredding the targets down range. It was to me invigorating, showing our skill and a warning to all, "don't mess with the Borne" or Canucks in general! Also, that week we had to do our annual 2 x 10-mile march. It was a standard qual. In Combat Arms, back to back 10 mile marches in full fighting order. Usually done by platoon, it was timed, the maximum being under two hours. I had a personal best time, something like 90 minutes. The final part of the training was a patrolling ex. at Dhekelia a British base. Then we returned to Nicosia and 10 Platoon celebrated New Years Eve with a private reserved club called the Rainbow Club, ran by two Swedish women. We got beastly drunk after a good dinner. Then some Greek Cypriots crashed our party. Fights broke out shortly after, ending with the interlopers being ejected.

It was a fun thing for me, a reminder of the time I had been a bouncer at Carleton University's Pub. The Greeks threw some trash cans down the stairs at us, which led to a street fight. 10 Platoon ended up chasing them off, sporadic fights going on for blocks before we returned to the club. The Swedes were grateful for our efforts, the party going on till first light. I laughed as I chatted with my old friends, most of whom I had fought with previously. Wadleigh, Farrell, Dorion, and Donny Foster. They all ended up being close friends and would back each other up to the death. We happy few...we band of brothers!

On January 2nd, we entered 1986, the last year of my posting to the Airborne and 3 Commando. For that month of January, it was routine patrolling and sentry duty on our sector of the Green line. On January 13, I received another pass for two days. Dave Farrell, Sergeant Lavery and I went off to Paphos for some more training with the British Freefall Club. I did two good exits and jumps, qualifying for my first freefall jump. Then on January 15th I went on my two weeks of U.N. leave. I chose Germany of course, boarding a plane that morning and leaving Cyprus behind for two weeks. We landed at Lahr base later that afternoon. Three of us rented a car, driving around Bavaria and ending up at a U.S. Base near Munich called Ulm. Gauthier one of my 3 Commando mates and a reservist visited Liz, an American from Texas whom we had met during our desert op. Liz was a beautiful young maiden, who acted as our German host for the next few days. Finally, as I had other places to see, I kissed her good-bye and headed off in the rental car. Next stop was Zurich, Switzerland for some downhill skiing.

Following the Autobahn south, it was an easy, pleasurable drive through the Alps to Switzerland. This must have been used throughout the millennia by ancient peoples, including the Romans who had used it to conquer all of Europe. History was evident everywhere, as the miles slid by and reached the capital of Zurich. Accompanied by the reservist, I parked the car and booked into a plush motel room. Of course it had a fridge stocked with booze, so I unwound by digging into it. After a shower, I dressed and hit the town, as my reservist friend stayed behind and slept. I laughed when he said he was tired from the drive. "Hello? McFly...I did all the driving! But I am Airborne...you are not. So sleep Leg!" It was a hectic but pleasurable night as I sampled Zurich's nightlife. I finally returned to the motel early that morning, getting a few hours sleep before hitting the famous ski slopes. It took the entire day to make it to the bottom, with a few stops at chalets for some rest and food.

Later that week, we returned to Bavaria, I dropped off my partner who was worn out by now. Then I drove north into the Rhine valley, finally stopping at Frankfurt. This was an ancient city, rebuilt after being flattened by Allied bombers during WW 2. I ended up in a big theatre, licensed and with a big stage, where a German band played. As a German waitress took my order, I noticed each table had a phone and a numbered ID card. As I drank from my large stein, the phone rang. I answered it, hearing a German female voice. Soon after she joined me, then we chatted and danced the night away. I drove her home, ending up at her apartment, where I met her half dozen female university friends. Also there was an American soldier. Well we hit it off, I was invited to stay as we drank the night away. I stayed there several days in the end. At one point it was so enjoyable, I mused about deserting the Canadian Army. My Yank buddy actually talked me out of it. "Y'all regret it in the end. We are both born warriors, so stick with it!"

Then I continued north, wishing them a good day, promising to return some time. I never did, hours later I crossed the Dutch border. I planned to visit the Arnhem Airborne memorials and cemeteries, where decades before in 1944, thousands of paras had died. It was surreal, seeing the long lines of tombstones. It sunk in how hazardous this Airborne thing was, how this had happened, a failure of intelligence leading to scores of young paratroopers dying in a just a few hours. "I hope you are in Valhalla my brothers. Some day I hope to join you!"

Stopping in Nijmegen, I met allot of Dutch, grateful for the sacrifice of many Canadians who liberated their country in 1944-45. I ended up in an all night bar, where the tenants were mostly gypsies. Initially they thought I was a German, as I was ordering my drinks in German, having acquired the language since being posted there in 1979. But after I convinced them I was a Canadian soldier, the gypsies befriended me. They bought me the odd round, even setting me up with a mysterious, beautiful woman. She was a great dancer, a bit older than me, but very talented. I was in her spell I felt, leaving with her to spend the night at her flat in the old part of the city. I hugged and kissed her goodbye the next day, then headed back for Lahr and my Canadian brothers. By the time my leave ended I was pretty much broke, but I was in high spirits. We partied the last hours in the town, visiting the Red-Light district, where one could get anything they wanted...nothing more may be said! Finally, my Herc taxi touched down in Cyprus after the two-week leave ended. It was like I awoke from a dream, as I dozed on the bus bringing my group of soldiers back to reality and Nicosia for duty. Back with 10 platoon that evening, I regailed my buddies with stories of my crazy, lightning tour of Europe. I did not know it then, but it was to be the last. Decades later, now in 2019, I still crave to return to carry on my tour. So many places to see, all of

Eastern Europe, which was out of bounds to us then in the 1980's. The Berlin wall fell in 1990, after my release from the Canadian Forces. Hopefully I will get the chance to see some of these exciting, historic places before my time is up.

As February arrived, I was relieved to know the U.N. tour was nearing its end. It was nose to the grind stone for the next month for the most part. Long sentry shifts throughout our sector of the Green line. On February 7- 9th a few of us freefall guys jumped for the last time on the island. My last of three jumps where my best to date, qualifying for my first freefall. However, I would not get the chance till after I returned to Canada. In fact, it was the following year in August of 1987, at Grand Bend, Ontario that I did my next civvy skydive. I had to repeat a refresher course, then in July of 1988 I finally did my first freefall jump. I was out of the army at this point, attending Fanshawe College in London, Ontario. I jumped out at 10,500 feet with my instructor Bob Wright that warm summer day over Georgian Bay. But more of this later.

Other than the routine sentry shifts, the men of 3 Commando continued to update our skills and participate in several sports competitions. One special training session involved the Ranger Swim test. Conducted at an indoor, Olympic sized pool, this test was designed by the U.S. Army Ranger Regiment. The test demanded a display of courage, jumping from a diving board wearing full combat equipment and personal weapons. Weighed down by the equipment, the soldier sank to the bottom of the pool. To pass and not drown, it required cool headedness, stripping off the equipment, while holding one's breath, then swimming up to the surface with one's rifle. It went smoothly for myself and the platoon, except for one guy. This NCO struggled at the bottom, then went unconscious, saved by the safety divers who were waiting for such an emergency. He was brought to the surface, dragged out and CPR performed. As we watched nervously, finally all were relieved to see him cough and spit out water. Later as we congratulated him he replied.

"I wasn't worried guys. I knew the platoon would have my back." It summed up the creed of paratroopers everywhere. The final part of this test was to swim a lap around the perimeter of the pool wearing full combat uniform and boots. It might sound nothing special, but it was a test of endurance, the soaked clothing and boots adding extra weight and drag. I finished it, sputtering and burnt as I climbed out of the pool. The U.S. Navy Seals and the Rangers have this test during their Selection phase, therefore it is of no surprise that the failure rate is high at over 50%.

Around this time, I was moved to 11 Platoon, an administrative move to balance the four platoons in 3 Commando. Another competition which had started in September, was the CANCONCYP "Around the Island Run." The goal was to run a minimum of 410 miles over the six-month tour of Cyprus. This was just another of many Airborne challenges, meant to inspire us to keep our standard of high personal fitness. In my case, I ran 3 miles on September 9, gradually lengthening the runs to 4,5,6,8,10 to 20 miles on the final day in February 28. My final total distance was 421 miles, exceeding the minimum by 11 miles. As an experienced paratrooper, I knew well that meeting the minimum was never good enough. After returning to Canada, I received a plaque as a memento of meeting this standard, along with the U.N. medal of service. I also was a member of the Commando rugby team and the soccer team. The rugby team played several challenge matches against U.K. Army teams. The one that sticks out was our match vs. The Welsh Guards rugby team. This is Wales national sport, therefore they had been playing since they were young children. For us Canucks, it was new, since we had formed the team the previous spring in Dundurn. It was a tough, hard hitting close match which the Welsh won by a hair. Since we were in prime condition, we managed to hold our own and gave the Welsh a good game as they told us. Having earned their respect, they subsequently invited us to their drinking mess for post game celebrations. It was a pleasurable event, drinking and singing Welsh army songs, becoming friends and brothers with our Welsh hosts.

Surprisingly our soccer team did even better. Playing several matches over the tour, we went undefeated, winning the Island's U.N. soccer competition. As a part of our winning team I received another memento, a gold medal for first place. Later back in Petawawa, our new CO, Major Ring told us he had met with his counterpart in 2 RCHA, our partner in the Cyprus tour. This officer, Lt. Colonel R.B. Mitchell the Commander of Sector 4, Canadian Contingent, had purchased a trophy cabinet to display all the trophies the Artillery would win. However, 3 Commando stole the show, winning every major competition except one. The RCHA C.O., humbled by their lack of success gave the trophy case to the Airborne after our return to our base camp. One of the challenges organized was an Obstacle course race, one of the Airborne's bread and butter training tools. The problem was when we got there, there was no obstacle course of note in existence on the island. So we constructed one in our off time. Then we challenged all comers and took first place. Also, adding to the Spartan facilities, we built the only Turkish sauna on our base. Many used it to relax after a long shift or PT training.

Before we left Cyprus, 3 Commando left its mark, leaving vastly improved facilities for subsequent tours. But I was most pleased that 3 Commando and the rest of the Canadian contingent had achieved its primary mission, to keep the tenuous peace on the island. Of course, 3 Commando was ill suited to this type of routine, peacetime service. As part of the Airborne, our primary mission was quick reaction, to fight anywhere in the world. U.N. Duty to us was a complete about face, meant for policemen or boy scouts. Sending highly trained, aggressive elite soldiers into this place, between two heavily armed aggressive armies armed with an unloaded gun and 20 rounds is asking for trouble. In fact, in my humble opinion, it is down right dumb, a purely political use of soldiers. But at the time we followed orders blindly.

THE FINAL DANCE

Finally, I returned to Canada in early March of 1986 on a chartered Boeing 737 jet. We landed at Ottawa's International airport, then began the final leg on buses to CFB Petawawa. I heard later, another jet carrying members of the U.S. 101st Screaming Eagles Division had crashed near Gander, Newfoundland. Several hundred of our American 'brother paratroopers' died that day, a reminder of the tenuous thread of life for all of us. Except for a twist of fate, it could easily have been my group on that plane. The investigators later said it was due to ice build up on the wings and control surfaces that caused the crash. It reminds one of that saying, "why jump from a perfectly serviceable airplane?" My response to these non-jumpers is, 'there ain't one. Well I am still here. How many have died landing in serviceable planes?"

After 3 Commando re-joined The Canadian Airborne Regiment at CFB Petawawa in February, we resumed our normal duties and training as we were plunged once more into Winter warfare training. This was basically refresher training for us, having repeated the same training for years, in my case going on eleven years. It was important however, getting accustomed to (acclimatizing) the freezing temperatures and working with new team mates. Of course, there was a host of administrative paperwork to finish our U.N. duty. Turn in gear not required back in Canada and reissued with our standard Airborne kit and weapons.

Some jostling of personnel occurred, some were promoted, some went on courses such as the Pathfinder, Ranger and Jump Master courses. On March 13, I returned to the jump scene, jumping from a CH-147 Chinook medium, dual rotor helicopter onto DZ Anzio outside of Petawawa. It was jump number 37, an administrative 'fun jump' meaning daylight, no equipment. I was the number one stick leader, a rare event for me. It was also a ramp jump and went smoothly. Later that evening I jumped again from the Chinook, this time #19 port at the back end of the stick. This was also fun, as the rear guys were running as they approached the ramp. Then one threw the static line and hurtled off the rear shouting Airborne. Jump # 38 was pleasurable, as I looked down at the panorama of the DZ below. The big main jerked open and I floated down to dear mother Earth in a state of near ecstasy. After landing, I lit up a cigarette and enjoyed the brisk walk back to the waiting DZ party to drop off my rig.

At this point I was aware my tour in the Airborne was nearing the end. That July I was slated to be rotated out, posted to one of the RCR's three infantry battalions. I did not really want to leave, so looked at alternatives to extend my stay in the Borne. The only way I heard was to 're-badge' to the PPCLI, who populated 2 Commando. I had several buddies in this unit, who suggested I talk to the CSM and the CO. They were open to my joining their unit, but I still had to get my CO Major Ring and the RCR to approve it. Of course, ultimately, they did not approve. I was told I was RCR and that was it. My future was written in stone, leaving in July for 1st Battalion, RCR.

In the meantime, I tried to get as many paratroop drops and specialized Airborne training as I could. In April, I jumped only once, #39 on April 29 slated at #9 port on the C-130. It was a night, full equipment jump followed by a distinctly hard landing on DZ Anzio. There was allot of range work in April, firing our main personal weapons. I was already a crack shot, particularly with the FN C1, 7.62 mm rifle. It was fairly heavy fully loaded with a 20-round magazine, also having a powerful kick. Later in the 1990's this standard issue rifle in the Canadian Forces was replaced by the lighter 5.56 mm C-7, based on the U.S. AR-15 semi-automatic rifle. Like the FN Belgian manufacturer, there was also a fully automatic version. That month I passed the rifle coaching course. Also my platoon I/C finally checked off the last objectives of the TQ-5 qualification. This meant I was qualified for the next rank of corporal. Long overdue in my opinion, as I was already a trained NCO, a veteran paratrooper/infantryman and had displayed leadership qualities on many occasions.

There are many qualities that make a good soldier. But to make a good, competent paratrooper even more is demanded. I found over three years in the Borne, that there was no limit to what I could achieve, if I could mentally push past those so called walls/barriers. Our goal was to succeed at any mission given to us. To push the envelope. Anything but first place did not count, no effort was ever the best, the individual trooper could always learn and do better. In May, I performed two more jumps, # 40-41. On the 18th it was an administrative fun jump at Anzio, from a CH-137 Twin Huey helicopter. At 1250 feet, the pilot slowly hovered above the drop zone. The side doors were open, the jump masters hooked our static lines to the floor, then we sat in the door. There were six/eight jumpers in the chopper, plus the JM and three flight crew. Given the green light, I stood on the landing skid below my feet, then simply pushed off. It was insane as I felt myself fall, as if I had just leapt off a high building.

There was none of the usual prop blast from the larger aircraft I was used to, which also were cruising near 200 knots. For 5-6 seconds, I stared down at the ground below, looming up at me. My hand rested on the reserve handle as I counted off the seconds, waiting for the big, round main to open.[7] Luckily so far, I never had to deploy my reserve, as I did not have a parachute malfunction. It remained in my thoughts however, reinforced by yearly refresher courses, designed to keep emergency procedures fresh in the mind of the paras. Back to the present jump, I felt a relief as the main chute cracked open overhead, with a gentle tug on the body shoulder and leg straps. I gasped in joy as I floated serenely down to the tiny figures below. "OMG! So, this is what I was missing! A freaking bare-ass baby jump!" After hitting the ground and rolling I had a feeling of euphoria wash over me. I patted the ground as I felt the relief and joy I experienced after every jump, for anyone could be your last ever!

A week later, on the 25th, it was back to the C-130 Herc. It was an administrative double door jump, where they manifested me at #14 port side stick. It was a standard, every day jump for the Airborne, still potentially hazardous, definitely not for everyone. It went smoothly, as we were by now a well-oiled team. We were also not carrying any extra weight and it was in daylight over the DZ. So to me, it was a piece of cake. After hitting the well known ground, it was routine business, pack up the chute, sling it over the shoulder and trot over to the RV to

---

[7] Later when doing civilian skydives and freefall, the jumper had an altimeter on the wrist to precisely gauge one's height. Army static line jumps were much simpler, the paratrooper had to count to gauge altitude.

drop it off, then stand around and have a smoke watching the other jumpers come in.

In June, I had my busiest month jumping, as a big Telex bivouac was going on in Petawawa. This was used to test new equipment, initiate our NATO Allies to Canadian Airborne jump procedures and aircraft, and give our 'administrative types' a few easy jumps to get current. Frequently paras are not current, meaning they have not jumped in over a year.

This could be due to injury, courses or foreign postings. To get current they had to take a refresher jump course (compressed into a day) before getting manifested for a jump. June 7th happened to be my last full equipment night drop. Jump # 42 was on DZ Anzio again. It was followed by a tactical, live fire exercise. 3 Commando as part of the Airborne Battle Group was tasked with doing a night march to the Petawawa River. We were given a full load of ammunition and each carried extra ammo for the heavy weapons (anti-tank, MG, mortars, radio batteries, mines and explosives). That spring our platoon had gone through the Explosives course, learning about the latest mines, C-4 explosives, fuses, booby traps and IED's. Also, we were all trained mountain warfare soldiers, so knew the basics of how to build rope bridges.

For the exercise, media photographers were attached to the Commandos. We did not converse with them, warned that anything we said would be in the papers the next day. So we kept silent, glaring at the civvy media guys, who just smiled and gave us the thumbs up as we trudged down the dirt tracks to the river crossing. After reaching it, men were detailed to construct a three-rope bridge over the fast-flowing Petawawa River. It was we knew a treacherous crossing, many having drowned in it over the decades. At first light the order was given to begin crossing. My section went over in assault boats, paddling directly below the three-rope bridge dangling overhead. I was perched near the back, wearing my combat webbing, rucksack, M-72 A/T launcher and rifle, loaded for bear. It was still black out as I peered ahead, as I sat on the rear of the assault boat. Then unexpectedly a dangling rope from the bridge snagged me under my chin. It almost dragged me over the back, as I struggled to untangle myself. I thought briefly if I went into that river, they would never see me. I would drown for sure, then I remembered the Ranger swim test, which we had done in Cyprus a few months before. I controlled my beating heart, then finally got the rope off. "Whew! That was tight! I almost fucking bought the farm," I hissed to a buddy in front.

Then the river was lit up by Para flares and the shit hit the fan. A C-2 gunner up front cut loose a burst at the far bank. This was answered by simulated artillery exploding in the water, smoke grenades and machine gun fire from the flanks. "Dig in boys! Hit that bank!" Every oar dug in harder as we surged toward the far bank. I pushed by the camera guy as we hit the shallow water, then leapt over the side. The enemy had put out a wire obstacle in the thigh high water, so we used pliers to cut a hole through it. A sergeant ordered a few of my group to carry the cameraman to the nearby bank so he did not get soaked...like we did.

At last we burst through the gap in the wire, taking up firing positions and locating the enemy positions. It was an adrenaline surge of activity as we rapidly moved in small teams, shouting out directions and distance to the enemy positions, well camouflaged trenches and bunkers. I was out in the lead when I hit the ground, taking cover behind some shrubs. I saw a large log bunker about 50 meters in front. My section commander then gave me the order to hit it with my M-72. I nodded as I knelt in the mud, stripping off my heavy ruck and unslinging the rocket launcher. With a range of 200 meters, it was one of my favourite toys. First to arm it, the end caps were taken off, then pressing a button, it was extended. This released the flip up sights. Then a look to the rear to check the back-blast area, as this was a recoilless weapon. "Clear!" I shouted to my section mates around me. Then balancing the rocket launcher over the shoulder, take a sight aim, flick the safety off, control the breathing and squeeze the trigger.

The 66-mm rocket spat out in a blast of high velocity smoke and flash. It hit the firer in the face like a slap from a fist. I blinked my eyes, then saw the explosion as the rocket hit the log bunker squarely ahead. A geyser of dirt and pieces of wood flew up in the air, amidst whoops of excited paras. I did not wait for the next order, throwing the one-shot M-72 away, grabbing my FN rifle and sprinting forward. I grabbed a grenade from my belt pouch with one hand as I reached the entrance to the smoking bunker, rounds cracking around me from my platoon. Then pulling the pin, I lobbed the grenade into the open doorway. I hit the bottom of a nearby trench for cover, then seconds later the grenade exploded with a dull crump.

The smoke and burnt cordite wafted through my nose as I struggled up, grinning at my mates watching from nearby. Then yelling bloody murder, I fixed bayonets and charged the smoking bunker. I fired two shots into the door, then bending down burst inside. It was dark and smoky in the bunker as my eyes adjusted to the hazy gloom, wiping sweat from my eyes. I saw two targets on the far wall, so instinctively took aim and fired off two shots into each. Then crossing the bunker, I lunged forward and bayoneted the riddled enemy targets. The bunker neutralized, I emerged after a minute or so to take stock. I watched as the platoon and others from 3 Commando manoeuvered forward, past the smoking bunker to finish off the enemy position. Overhead we noticed Huey choppers with their lights on, hovering over the river nearby. A short time later, the assault over our platoon regrouped back at the river.

We took sips of water as our throats were parched dry from the assault. We discussed the choppers, wondering why their lights were on. This was simulated war, therefore it was strictly against the rules, except if something was badly wrong. It turned out that a new guy, from 2 Commando who had been crossing the three-rope bridge had fallen into the raging river below. A short time later 2 Commando was stood down from the exercise to search for the missing soldier. For the rest of the Airborne though it was carry on and finish the mission. We accepted this, for this is what would happen in combat. There is no time to grieve for lost men.

We advanced to contact our enemy force over the next two days, practicing our procedures, drills and speed of movement. Finally End-Ex was called after we assaulted the last enemy position, storming up the long slope of a ridge. It was strewn with obstacles to hinder us, wire obstacles, mine fields and such. The first guys would hurdle themselves over the wire, while the rest of us climbed over his body. We also constructed make shift ladders to throw over high obstacles. It was like a large obstacle course, emphasizing team work, leadership, communication and Airborne spirit. The C.O. complemented us afterward during the debrief. Then we were told the missing lad from 2 Commando had been found the final day. He had drowned, his body loaded down with gear had floated down the river for quite a way. It was a sombre end to an otherwise successful exercise. It would be my final act in the Airborne play.

Posted: 1 RCR CFB London, Wolseley Barracks

At the end of June, I got my orders along with a half dozen of my 3 Commando buddies to clear off Petawawa base and report to 1 RCR in London. It was sort of sad after three years in the Airborne Regiment. The worst effect it had was to end a very promising, long term relationship I had with a young woman. I had met her, Miss Suzie Keefe through Airborne mates. In fact, her cousin Brian I knew was in the elite Pathfinder platoon. I was introduced formally at a bar in Ottawa, surrounded by several Airborne soldiers. So in the spring of 1986, as my three-year term attached to 3 Commando was coming to the end, I knew the Army system in Canada dictated I would be posted to one of the RCR's three regular force infantry battalions. I talked this over with Suzie, we were in love I believe. We had been an item for over a year, at this point

I had not proposed or formally engaged. I had met her parents at their home in Aylmer, Quebec I believe. I got along with her father, who was an officer in the Canadian Forces. They were an upper middle class family, at this time I believe she was an university student. As we got to know each other, I said I had been a student at Carleton University in Ottawa, prior to joining the Regular Army in 1983.

My goal at the time, was to get an extension in the Airborne Regiment. I informed the OC of 3 Commando, Major Leavy, who had been my commanding officer since I joined the unit. He looked into it, but ultimately my request was rejected. I next talked to my friends in 2 Commando, whose parent unit was the PPCLI. They encouraged me to rebadge to their regiment, if successful, I could be transferred to 2 Commando, thus remaining in Petawawa with the Airborne. I talked to both the CSM and the OC, both of who accepted my request. They sent the paper work for approval by the RCR. For some reason, never explained to me, the transfer was denied. It was written in stone, I was an RCR soldier and would remain one. No other option was available, I would go in July to 1 RCR in London, Ontario. In June knowing this, I was in a depressed mood, then informed my girl friend. I asked her what she wanted to do. She said she could not move with me, so our relationship ended abruptly.

However it was exciting as well, a new challenging experience. In the Canadian Forces, this was routine, particularly in Combat Arms (Infantry, Armour, Artillery). Each of the Regular Force Regimental battalions were strung out across Canada and abroad. One way of spreading Airborne skill and expertise was to rotate men in and out every three years. Others like the American and U.K. Airborne/Paras used a far different approach from ours. An individual paratrooper once they had made the grade, could stay their entire career in the mother unit, the Airborne. Of course, if they really excelled, they could apply for Special Forces.

But in the 1980's Canada had no Special Forces units as such. The Airborne as the tip of the spear of the SSF Brigade was it. As I was to find out soon, the Regular Infantry was a step backward, the training not nearly as challenging or exciting for the most part. It had its moments of course, particularly during the annual RV Divisional level exercises. Technically the Special Force Brigade soldiers should have been all Airborne qualified and Commandos.

In reality, there were only a few amongst a battalion of over 500 men. However, over the next year I managed to jump four more times, as the Airborne was at that time under strength. On the last day of June, I finished clearing out of 3 Commando and CFB Petawawa, loaded up my Mustang and headed across Ontario for London. I pit stopped at my family home in Plantagenet to update the folks and get a descent home cooked meal. I had mixed emotions as I told my parents and family sitting out having a beer on the front porch. I had survived the three-year posting to the Airborne. I had passed the rigorous selection, attained my jump wings and seen the world, so to speak. I was turning a corner now, entering the next phase of my life and military career. It was starting to bother me a bit though, waiting on my promotion. I must have been one of the most heavily trained privates on the planet. What would it take for the Army to make such a drastic move? Only the gods knew that I joked.

In the first week of July, I arrived finally at Wolseley Barracks, London in southern Ontario. One of my Airborne buddies was with me then. Rick Dorion was a younger soldier, we having served in 10 Platoon for the bulk of my time in the Borne. Having some time left, we went to Wasaga Beach, north of London on Georgian Bay. He assured me the place was packed with hordes of women from the Toronto area. He knew of course I had lost my girlfriend as well as my status as an Airborne soldier. He was probably trying to help me to get over the loss. After swimming and checking out the beach, we bar hopped the area, relaxing and talking over what 1 RCR had to offer. "Well I am single again Rick. Broke off things with Suzie before I left. She did not want to relocate here. Sad eh?"

"Ah relax dude. There are hordes of available chicks here to snap you up." Dorion was from a well off Toronto family as he had said. The opposite of me, who was raised on a farm until 16, before relocating to Ottawa and attending Carleton University. On July 3, we cleared into Wolseley Barracks at the duty office. The Duty Officer, a young lieutenant, informed us the battalion was on leave for two weeks. He gave us an offer which most of us, fresh from the Commando took. In exchange for working on the Connaught Rifle range near Ottawa for a few weeks, we would take 2 weeks leave after. I travelled there in my Mustang with a few of the guys and worked on the range staff for the next week. I was used to this, a part of the routine, fairly easy duty. Then we got notice to return immediately to London. Apparently the CSM of our company, D Company, or Dukes Company as it was termed, wanted us back urgently.

As it happened, my Mustang was in the shop, getting a new engine update. My older brother Mike said he could help me out, installing a rebuilt 302 V-8. He had put in the previous 6-cylinder engine, which I blew shortly after getting to the ranges. I asked the range Warrant Officer if it was OK to extend me for another week till my car was fixed. He later told me this was fine, as he needed my services anyway. There was a big rifle competition that week, so I was busy working on the range. Finally, a week or so later, with my Mustang back and handling very nice, I returned to London near the end of August. When I cleared onto Wolseley Barracks I was told to report to the CSM's office. My first thoughts were, "Ah good! My promotion finally!" Then I saw the new CSM as I halted before his desk and had an ominous feeling. He looked like a Leg (Airborne term for non-jumpers) and a paper pusher. He stared up at me with his thick glasses, not a hint of a smile on his face. It did not faze me much, as I focussed over his head at the far wall. I knew from experience, that long term RCR personnel were committed to one thing or God, the RCR. This was typical in most regiments, my paratrooper status meant little here. But they must want me here I thought, why force me to transfer here in the first place?

"Private Gilligan reporting Sir!" He asked me why I was late reporting, as he had ordered me back over a week before. Then he said that I had disobeyed his orders and was on an AWOL charge (meaning absent without leave). I told him my superior, the W.O. had OK'd it and had permission to stay on the range till the competition was finished. This fool, surprisingly a Sergeant Major did not buy it. I was marched before the Company O.C. shortly after. After checking out my story, the charge was of course thrown out, but this idiot, the CSM did not let it go, staying on my back, continually trying to find some fault with the performance of my duties. Apparently, he had a vendetta against airborne, serving or anyone like myself who had been Airborne. Why I asked myself many a day, and how was he promoted to CSM? I heard another Senior NCO, who knew this person when he was young. He had gone on a jump course and failed it. He took it personally like most losers, using his rank to go after successful soldiers.

I also learned during subsequent field exercises, that CSM Twatley, (my nickname for him), did not care for the field. "Seriously? He is CSM of an Infantry Company! This is our bread and butter! What will he do if we go into a combat Op?" So he did not attend our many field training exercises, preferring to stay safe and warm in his office and working a nine to fiver. I lost all respect for the Sergeant Major at this point and we developed a nice hatred for each other.

I invited him to 'step behind the wall' to settle our differences like men. Not being a fighter, he declined of course, choosing to hide behind his rank. This was the 1980's, when disputes where settled physically. So I continued to be a target, finally I asked to be transferred out of his company after a few months. This was refused, the lame excuse being they could not afford to lose a trained soldier like me. So why was I getting the rookie 'new guy' treatment? That fall was course time, I indicated my choices, being ADP or Pioneer training. These were particularly suited to me and my future as an infantryman. ADP (Armour Defence Platoon) and Pioneer (Engineers) demanded trained personnel, I having the basics in both over a decade of army experience. Again, the CSM stuck his face in though, declining all my requests and relegating me to a Radio Comms course.

"Sergeant Major did you read my personal file? I have already taken a radio course years ago." He replied it did not count as it was in the reserve force. I said I was a senior private and due for a course of my choice. But the thick-headed CSM waved off my argument, telling me it was his way or the highway. If this dolt knew what I was thinking as I marched out, he would have called the MPs or the police. I was in a very dark mood, fighting off impulses to do something nasty to the freak. I drowned my sorrows in the mess that night, heading off to a bar with my ex-Airborne buddies Dorion and McGean. It helped me to right the ship, returning my good morale as they calmed me down, buying rounds and telling filthy army jokes.

The Radio course proceeded that week, boring the crap out of me, as I sat in the room listening to some Leg blather on about trivial radio procedures. In the end I passed it easily, telling the CSM and others it was a good refresher, something like a para refresher. This of course needled the CSM, as I knew it would, being a failure on his basic para. Having got my Comms qualification, I never touched a radio again. I was already planning my future then, I put in a formal request to be posted out, preferably to the Airborne. It was rare for the Army to see this, also being a slap in the face to said mother unit the RCR. Over the next year, I redressed their refusal, also a demand for a remuster to another trade. Thanks to idiots like that CSM, I had finally reached the end of my tether in the infantry. As I said later to the battalion CO, "Transfer me Sir or I am not resigning. I will not stay here another day more than I have to."

I did have several allies in the battalion, including the RSM Irvine, who had been my CSM in 3 Commando. The following year I was finally promoted to Corporal in the spring of 1987. Also, that spring, while on a Battalion parade, I received my CD for twelve years' service. It was my third medal to go with my wings, more than anyone in Dukes Company, except for a few Senior NCO's. Most were young soldiers fresh off their basic training.

My section commander had never been on a field exercise or a foreign Op. Like his mentor, the CSM, inexperienced yet proudly arrogant. I said it then, if we were to go to war, our company would perish in the first hours or run for the hills. It was meant as a joke, but no one laughed, including me. It was pathetic and would lead to my Honourable Release that July. I was humiliated to be in this 'old folks home' as it was termed. During a PT run, the 'ex-Airborne' soldiers were put in the rear, because our pace would lose most of the out of shape soldiers following us. The best part of that final twelve year run in the Army was an occasional jump with the Borne. I was told it was not the same, so do not rush back. Apparently, the officers had lowered the strict standards and downsized the Borne to an understrength battalion from a Regimental Battle Group.

In other words, the writing was on the wall, so it helped me to decide and release from the Forces in July of 1987. Five years later the Airborne met its Waterloo, during the ill-fated Somalia UN Operation. Having lowered their standards, doing away with the AIC course, several troublesome low quality soldiers entered the Commandos. Charged with the murder of a Somalian thief, the bad press mounted up. Shortly after returning to Canada in the mid 1990's the presiding Liberal government disbanded the Airborne Regiment in disgrace. At that time, I had finished a College level program in Science, while still in London. I moved to Mississauga in the fall of 1990, working with an Environmental air quality testing firm till laid off in the following spring of 1991, then moved back to Ottawa once more. I worked in Public Service Labs as I tried to adjust to civilian life. It was not easy, most civilians at the time shunning anyone with a military background, thinking we were still in Vietnam. I was even asked if I had gone there. I heard things like, "How many babies have you killed?"

But back to London and 1 RCR. Having given up on returning to the Borne, I planned my future moves. I started a diary in Cyprus, keeping notes on my army experiences. It was my family who put the idea of becoming a writer in my head, but it was not till decades later before writing in earnest. In May of 1987, my unit, 1^s Battalion of the RCR shipped out for Wainwright, Alberta for Rendezvous Exercises, known as RV 87. My company

D 'Dukes' Company, was first tasked with constructing a large defensive position. It was modelled after a Russian company sized defensive position, which would then be used in live fire attack. It was the CSM I heard, who volunteered us for this monumental work. It took us several weeks of back breaking work under the Alberta heat, digging trenches, bunkers, cutting wood, filling sandbags and such.

Finally, we had it inspected by a group of high ranking officers, our CSM finally appearing as if by magic. I joked with my mates, that since he resembled a rodent, maybe he had just popped out of a groundhog hole! They doubled over with laughter, as this is what soldiers do in the field. We make jokes, often at other's expense. MY young section commander did not see the humour, warning us to show respect for our leaders. I stared at this fellow, asking who he was referring to. "Leaders? You don't mean that fat desk clerk over there, trying to look important to the Generals? Where was he for past two weeks? Leading from his comfortable barracks miles behind the lines." Later my mates suggested the young section commander probably relayed my comments to the CSM afterwards.

That we (Dukes Company) did not see the CSM during this period, is how one gets promoted I thought. Be present for the big wigs and talk a good fight. As our self-anointed leader led the officers around our finished defensive works, it was pronounced ready. D Company attacked it over the next few days, all live fire. Of course, the CSM was nowhere to be seen, as this was serious soldiering and dangerous work. One could be injured or killed fairly easily. During the last attack, my section (8-10 men) attacked one section of the defensive position, with mortars exploding to the front, machine guns firing from our flanks in support. The air was filled with smoke, the noise deafening, we could feel shock waves hitting our bodies from explosions, the whine and crack of bullets, missiles and shrapnel whizzing nearby. After working our way to the nearest trench, we heaved grenades inside, then moving in teams entered the trench. As I jumped in, loaded down with weapons and ammo, my foot caught on the sandbag wall. All my weight came down on it, twisting my ankle, then I felt it snap audibly.

"Shit! My ankle is broke...keep going guys! I will stay here and support." I fired over the trench at a nearby bunker as the rest of the section fought their way toward it. After capturing the position, I was helped back to the rear. It was painful as a medic examined my leg, taking off my combat boot.

"Looks like a sprain or a fracture. We must X-ray it back at the field hospital." The medic informed me, then wrapped my ankle before I was loaded into an ambulance. Also during that assault, M/Cpl MacDonald who was with my platoon in the Airborne the last three years was wounded by a ricochet, probably a rifle bullet striking one of the metal plates used as targets inside the Russian defensive position. He was acting as a Safety umpire, standing to the rear of the assaulting troops. It hit him in the shoulder, not life threatening, but like myself, putting him out of action for the time being.

At the field hospital later, x-rays confirmed my ankle was in fact fractured. So, I was out of the field, probably for the duration of RV-87. The doctor told me over the next day or so he would order MacDonald and myself returned to London on the next available plane. After returning from the hospital, the sick and wounded reported to the CSM for 'sick parade.' I stood before him, leaning on my crutches as he assigned our daily routine duties. I was told I would be assigned to the kitchen staff, for the remainder of RV 87. I shook my head, smiling at his grim face. There was no sense of camaraderie between us, which is typical in good army units. The fact I had been injured doing my job in a hazardous environment meant little to him, nor were my high level of expertise and training He had not been there, his goal already attained in "Brown nosing" to the senior officers the day before. I was just a little pawn he used to push across the board, in his little world. Luckily this was peacetime training, not real war.

"Sorry Sir, I am afraid that will not be happening. The Chief medical officer has given me light duties, till I return to London." He was not in agreement, repeating that I would report for duty to the cooks. "Yes sir!" I was dismissed and hobbled off, making a bee line to the hospital tent. I told the M.O. what the CSM had ordered, asking him to confirm it. The M.O. subsequently ordered the CSM to report, telling the CSM he could not override his order, as he out-ranked him. The flustered CSM tried to argue his right to control his man, but after being threatened with charges, quickly backed off. I thanked the officer, watching with pleasure as my hated nemesis slinked off. He told me that if he harassed me any further, to report to him. I saluted and left, pleased that for now at least, the CSM was prevented from making my life hell. A few days later, the plane arrived, a Hercules, my trusty taxi from the Airborne days.

My buddy MacDonald joined me, both of us in good spirits as the plane lifted off the runway for the long trip back to London. We talked during the long trip about home, he was finally tying the knot, getting married to his fiancée. I congratulated him, then lay back on the stretcher and slept the rest of the way. We touched down in London, arriving at the base hospital shortly afterward. It was a slow recovery over the next week, with the usual hospital routine, daily exams and starting rehab programs with trained nurses and staff.

Finally into the third week, the doctor told us we were doing well, offering to discharge us for a week of medical leave. We were overjoyed, shouting for joy at getting out of hospital. I said goodbye to Mac, then drove to Ottawa to spend some time at home with the folks. It was the best rehab, visiting my brothers and friends, drinking copious amounts of alcohol and telling war stories.

Finally, as the days flew by, it was time to return to London. Back at Wolseley Barracks, I parked my Mustang outside the duty office and reported in, still on my crutches. The duty Sergeant then informed me Mac was dead. I was stunned, in disbelief I asked how. He was a mentor and a friend, an Airborne brother and deemed virtually indestructible. The NCO said it was a boating accident on a fishing trip. He was with another RCR soldier, drinking as he sat in the small boat. He fell over the bow, submerged as the motor boat surged over him. When he came to the surface, his head hit the propeller, killing him instantly. I met his fiancée during the wake, giving my condolences. After the funeral, we were invited to their house for drinks. I was standing by the door, when Mac's pet parrot flew across the room and landed on my head.

It loosened up a rather tense, subdued atmosphere, as I joked about Mac getting in his last two cents. It was a sad day though, but as we dealt with his loss, I told myself this was a part of life. For the only two certainties in life were death and taxes. Small consolation to his loved ones though, so I left them to deal with their loss in their own way. For me I hooked up with my new girl friend, visiting bars with a horde of her female friends. After days of heavy drinking and parties, slowly Mac's sudden death eased from my mind. Wash away the old...in with the new. As I continued to rehab, I was coming up to an important cross-road in my army career. After the latest incident with the CSM, I was convinced I could not stay another year in that swine's paternal control. I had tried to accommodate his wishes, knowing that he despised the ground I trod on, and vice versa. After exhausting all efforts to get out of D Company, I had to decide, should I stay or should I go? That July was the end of my contract. To stay in the Forces, I had to 're-up' for the long haul, a decade or more to get a full pension.

The RCR wanted me to stay, so I had to spend another two years in London. I discussed it with my buddies and friends, most advising me to stay the course. I was getting paid more after my promotion, so at last I could buy a house, one of my long-term goals. I do not recall what finally decided it, probably nightmares about further incidents with the CSM. Frustrated at being denied his fun in Wainwright, I felt he was planning his next attempt to make my life as difficult as he could. Already he was trying to reduce my annual leave days, saying he had been perusing my personal record back to my Airborne tour. He had tried in vain to stop my promotion, then saying I would not receive my CD medal. He failed both times, but he was as stubborn as a mule. Finally I asked, "Why should I stay in an army that tolerates this obvious harassment, not only that, rewards it, promoting this low-quality infantry soldier?"

These were my parting words to the C.O. of the RCR battalion. I am getting out of this zoo Sir, I do not deserve this after twelve years of solid service. Send me to the Borne were I belong, replace some new guy who does not even want to serve there. I used all my powers of common sense to promote my argument. But this idea again fell on deaf ears, so I walked away, leaving the Army for good. Normally if a soldier does this, the Army treats him like garbage. Assigns him to boring, monotonous duties no one else wanted, or digging ditches, cleaning up garbage. But I had timed it right, leaving Wolseley Barracks next day after turning in my issued kit. That day, I returned to civilian life, thinking I could return at an appropriate time. I looked into taking a program at Western University, to complete my Bachelor of Science degree, begun at Carleton University in Ottawa in the 1970's.

I landed a spot at an upscale apartment in north London and finished my preliminary application to school, after returning home to pick up my academic records. It was a surreal confusing time after my release from the Army. Suddenly like hitting a wall, the stress and daily pressure vanished. I felt free for once, but still felt remorse and regret for leaving the life of a warrior and soldier. As a civilian now, a whole new way of life and rules replaced the Army's rigid system.

I slowly came to grips with my new life, thinking to myself, I can re-sign if civvy life does not agree with me. Nothing lasts forever anyhow. My family had mixed reactions, but my sweet heart was happy at least. Many a promising relationship had failed over those twelve years, due to the extensive periods of being far away, training, overseas ops or posted to a new base.

Also I had my latest love by my side, my Ford Mustang. The cowboys of the world know this, one relies and depends on your ride. Without one, you are stranded, ultimately leading to one's end. The boys in Custer's 7th Cavalry last thoughts were probably, "General let's mount up and get the hell out of Injun country!" No matter what mental state I was in over the past decades, a ride in my vehicle would quickly restore me to a normal state of morale. I have pretty much held the same mental approach my entire life.

One thing the army had taught me, was I loved to travel, rarely settling in one place for too long. We lived the life of a gypsy in that fashion. This allowed me in a way, to see the big picture, of how the world turned. Politicians tell one, diversity is strength. How many Canadian citizens actually practice this? I knew one fellow student in London, who had never left the city limits in two decades of his life or so. I had been born in Kingston, Ontario, moved to Napanee within a week, then on to Toronto metro area. I had my first accident there, first stitches in my head after falling off my tricycle. I threw my first punch, when the doctor asked if it hurt to pull at my cut skull. My father joked about that for years, he said I was a man of few words. Action was my way of answering the doc's naïve question. At three or so, I was on the move again. This time to a farm in Eastern Ontario. Our family farmed here for a decade or so, moving to another farm, in the Ottawa River valley. Then at 16, I left the farm for Ottawa after finishing high school. There I began university at Carleton, enrolled in the Army reserve and began life in earnest. Then after several years, in my early twenties, I signed up for the Regular Forces.. When I told this young student that, he laughed and said he did not need it.

My first big decision was, should I go to Western and stay in London for the next few years? Or return to home in the Ottawa area and finish my studies at Carleton U.? I never set eyes on my hated nemesis again as it turned out. I had dreams of it, meeting him in a dark place, with no one around to protect him. Like the ancient Greeks, or Vikings, a fight to the death. No quarter asked, none given. But this is modern society is it not? It remains one of those what ifs. I still regret that decision, even though it was probably the right and legal alternative.

Conclusion

So, what did I achieve from serving twelve years, the best years of my life in Canada's Armed Forces? Truthfully, I can say in good conscience I achieved allot and retain many valuable skills in the process. There were many positives and negatives of course. I knew many good soldiers who failed at being soldiers. It is not easy duty, especially in my trade, the infantry, or to use the American term the grunts, or the ground pounders. Canada has been slow in adapting to modern warfare, disbanding units like 1st Canadian Parachute Battalion, The Canadian Airborne Regiment and fully mechanized infantry. We had one brigade in Europe in the 1970-80's, but this was disbanded and all NATO bases closed by the 1990's. We also had another elite unit, our version of the British S.A.S. in the 1950's, but again was disbanded by our political leaders.

Many army veterans have been wounded, mentally or physically, some for life, others paying the ultimate sacrifice. I had several injuries, but I luckily escaped with my body and mind primarily in one piece. I had served during the Cold War era, so had missed my ultimate calling, serving in combat against the USSR. I have heard recently that close to 3000 veterans in Canada are living on the streets. Why have these heroes fallen through the cracks of our Veteran's programs? I do not have the answer to that, but I know if I was not battling for survival, with the help of some caring individual Canadians and planning for the future, I might be in their place. As a result, I should be thankful I have survived, own my own home and still have a life. Some who have not continued any physical fitness program after releasing from the Forces, abandoning the skills learned during their service, are treading a dangerous tight rope.

After my release in 1987, I still had skills, such as the basic freefall training in Cyprus. In the fall of 1987 I returned to the skies, one month after my release from the Canadian Forces, jumping at Grand Bend, on the shores of Georgian Bay, Ontario. My new instructor and mentor in the sport was the owner Bob Wright, who still runs the DZ to this day. It was enjoyable and relaxing for me, a stress reducer and gave my life purpose. I was made for it, as danger, excitement and adrenaline rushes were part of my life by now. Why jump from a perfectly serviceable airplane folks? If you don't know I can't explain it to you.

On August 13, 1987, I jumped at Grand Bend, Ontario. It was my seventh skydive, after the six in Cyprus. It was a static line refresher jump from a Cessna 182, the smallest jump plane in the world. I used a Falcon main chute (296 sq. ft.), climbing out the door to balance on the wheel strut. I was told to grab the wing strut in front, push off and look at Bob beside me. Bob climbed out after me on the wheel strut, holding the ripcord in his hand. When I was set, I looked over at his smiling face, he nodded and I pushed off and arched. As I looked up after releasing, arching and falling to the DZ 3000 feet below, the chute opened after four seconds. The main chute opened with a crack, leaving me to float serenely over the earth. It was a round chute but had toggle steering lines, so I could steer it to a selected landing spot. Also as a student, I carried a radio, linked to an instructor below, who advised me on landing procedures.

As the 80's decade rolled on, I was somewhat hampered by cash flow, as I was a full-time student and had no permanent job to rely on. Before graduating from college in 1990, I had nineteen civilian skydives, a dozen being freefall jumps, to go with fifty military jumps. My first freefall jump occurred on July 10, 1988, from 10,500 feet at Grand Bend. I exited the C-182 that day, followed by Bob and a second instructor Ken Watson. It was my first PFF jump (progressive freefall), practicing my arch, leg extensions, altimeter checks (for height awareness) and pulling the pilot chute to open the main. The freefall lasted 45 seconds, my terminal speed reaching over 120 mph. The two instructors held my harness from the sides as I went through the drills. I jumped three times in August and five in September, gradually adding more things (turns, moving forward and back/front flips).

It was different from military parachuting, so it took a change in mental approach, the planes, the parachute rig, the freefall speeds, more in flight manoeuvers and of course the landings. I learned to stay loose, practice on the ground and staying cool. The landings where the most challenging, eventually though, I got the timing right and stood up. This was a big 'no no' in military parachuting, due to the higher landing speeds and carrying heavy loads. So, once I nailed the landings, everything got much easier. On May 21, 1989, I did my nineteenth jump at Grand Bend. It was from the little C-182 again, this time from 7500 feet. It was a 15 second delay, as I practiced doing back loops. I got some hell for pulling at 5000 feet, as I forgot to check my altimeter. I landed OK though on the DZ, as it turned out my last ever at this DZ. I would not jump again till eleven years later. I received an offer in Toronto after graduation from my course at Fanshawe College, received my science diploma, then moving to the town of Brampton in the fall of 1990. I changed jobs a few months later, moving to nearby Mississauga.

One of my favourite sporting activities at this time was rugby. Having fallen in love with it during the Cyprus tour, I joined the city of London team in 1988. Unfortunately, I cracked my sternum in a scrum, being a prop in the front row. It was cartilage, so the doctors could do nothing. I could not play till the following year, or parachute, so it was hit the books. In 1990 I joined the Oakville Crusader Rugby squad, it being in the suburbs of Toronto Metro area. This became a full-time activity, practicing several times a week and playing a game on the weekends. Each member also had to pay his own club dues and buy all the equipment, except for the team jersey. It was intense, the most physically demanding game I ever played. Why do it? It changed my world for the next decade. I played for the Crusaders until the following year in 1991, everything blew up. An economic slump slowed my employer's business, ultimately leading to my being laid off. It was a nasty wake-up to the civilian world. I then moved back to Ottawa, working in labs for the Federal Public Service for the next decade.

I joined the Ottawa Scottish Rugby Club in 1992, playing in the scrum second row as a flanker. It was a natural spot for me, being a linebacker in football previously. In 1996 my team won the City of Ottawa championship, going undefeated during the season. Then it was back to university at Carleton U. I received a Bachelor of Science in 1998, shortly after becoming a self-employed consultant in Earth science. It was a grind as I learned the business over the next two years. I did not hear a gun shot or see a plane ride until one day in 2000. I had moved from Ottawa to Manitoba, staying briefly near my sister's acreage in Winnipeg, before getting an apartment in the city. I landed a job at CFB Shilo, doing meteorological work for the German Army. One hot summer day, on July 28 as my team sat in the radar bunker, I heard about this DZ north of Winnipeg. "Hey guys, let's go jumping!" That weekend I travelled north to the DZ at Gimli. I showed them my jump book, but I had to start with a basic jump first.

It went well, my thoughts were, "Will I still enjoy it?" It was sort of like riding a bike, the instincts and reactions stay in your sub-conscious memory. Eleven years after my last jump in Grand Bend, I did a hanging exit off the wing of the Cessna 182. It was a repeat of the Basic jump course, as I did not have a license yet. It went as planned, landing on my feet in the target zone. I did seven skydives in that year, the last a freefall from 4000 feet. It was also my first emergency, as I had a problem with the pilot chute, the AAD activated at around 1000 feet and landed under the reserve. The lesson learned was pay attention to altitude and checking the pilot chute ripcord was packed properly. It was intense and my first near miss, as things could have gone south rather quickly. That was it till the following year, in July when I switched DZ to Steinbach, Manitoba where I jumped five times, perfecting the basic skills.

Then in 2002, I moved to Edmonton, Alberta, to work in the Oil & Gas Industry, using my B.Sc. in Earth Science and Chemistry strengths. I started skydiving in June at the first DZ I found in Eden North, west of the city of Edmonton. The following year, after doing fifteen skydives and passing the basic drills, I qualified as a solo jumper. I relocated to Westlock DZ in August 2003, where I would do hundreds of skydives over the next fifteen years. I attained a B CoP license, bought my own jump gear and committed to a life of skydiving. It helped to keep me grounded, tests my mental and physical abilities, giving me a deep sense of purpose and confidence. I credit this ability to facing death with a cool demeanor with keeping me balanced over the worst of times. I have lost girl friends, jobs, friends, been assaulted and fined for various traffic offences. If a man loses his sense of self, something to hold onto, that gives him a sense of pride, one can lose his battle for life. Once this is gone, like a leaf floating in the breeze, one is at the whim of 'the gods.' As the Vikings knew, as well as ancient Greeks, there is no afterlife in Valhalla for the failed warrior.

I was injured again in 2017, my worst ever injury as a result of parachuting, when I borrowed a main chute, attached it to my rig, as a rigger was replacing the suspension lines on my main Sabre 190 chute. On the negative side, I fractured my left tibia and both wrists, was knocked out with a concussion, spending seven weeks in Royal Alex Hospital in Edmonton, undergoing surgery three times. It was the worst experience ever, resigned to depending on nurses as I lay in bed helpless. I relied on visits by two of my skydiving buddies, Travis McBride and his girlfriend. There were a few others, but Travis and Ana visited me several times, even sneaking me packs of cigarettes and later beer. It raised my morale immensely, after three weeks or so I was begging the doctors to get me out. They resisted my pleas and rightly so. As I was not married, I had no one to take care of me once I was released. I finally learned I would not be released until I could prove I could walk on crutches. This was a challenge, as I had casts on both arms until next February. However I overcame this liability, by badgering the doctors to let me have a go at the crutches. I was able to walk for the first time in mid October.

The story of the famous British Spitfire pilot during the Battle of Britain, Douglas Bader inspired me during this time. He had crashed before the war during one of his airplane test stunts, losing both of his legs. He eventually learned to walk again, despite the doctor's protests to the contrary. His stubborn nature, 'never say die' attitude and understanding wife propelled him to overcome his liability. Then he went on to learn to fly again. When the war began in 1939, he applied for entry into the RAF. He was refused entry, but as the war progressed, Britain was losing the battle. Then threatened directly after the fall of France, Hitler began his plan to invade his last surviving enemy. The Battle of Britain began and needed all hands-on deck. So, Bader won his battle, becoming squadron leader of a Canadian Spitfire squadron.

After winning over his undisciplined Canadians, he led them into becoming a stalwart of Britain's defences. After winning the battle, Bader continued the fight into occupied France. A year later, he was ambushed by Luftwaffe Messerschmitt fighters, shot down and captured. He lost one of his artificial legs after parachuting from the burning plane. Imprisoned in a German POW camp, he badgered the Germans into allowing an RAF plane to fly him in a replacement leg. After sorting this out, he attempted his first escape the next night, but was promptly captured and returned to the camp. He continued to be a thorn in the side of his enemy until the end of the war. This is a story I love to hear, true heroism in the face of defeat and death. I spent the next year after my release from hospital rehabbing, but my military experience and discipline helped me to overcome these obstacles and recover fully.

Another big, important skill I retained from the Canadian Forces was use of firearms and being comfortable with weapons, not a natural ability for many people. After being away from it for years, I returned to the firing range in 2018, while rehabilitating from my latest injury. After seven weeks and three surgeries, I did not know if I would ever parachute again. Hence as a back up plan, I purchased my first gun the following spring. I took my Alberta firearms licence and fired at the Phoenix indoor rifle range in March of 2017. Being an accomplished marksman, sniper and competent in a wide variety of weapons, it was like riding a bike. Also, gifted with above average eyesight, I was amazed at how accurate my first shots were. Once an avid outdoorsman and hunter, I used my new rifle on the Edmonton Base ranges, to learn my new weapon's characteristics and hone my abilities with it. For me to surrender this weapon, my foes will have to pry it from my cold, dead hands. In this I am with the Americans, as it is instilled in the American Constitution, the right to bear arms.

It has been years since my first parachute jump and decades since I was sworn in as an active serviceman in Canada's Armed Forces. It changed my life forever, something that has made me into what I am today. I have discussed this with many other soldiers, or warriors as some Americans call themselves. After a decade plus of active service, most would say they are soldiers forever, although technically civilians, it stays in one's brain forever. I can confidently say I would not have survived to this day without the many skills and experiences accumulated during my service. I have had many accidents, close calls with death and injury. Somehow, I have survived, while others perish in their first dangerous situation. Why, I have asked myself on many occasions. Part of it is luck, or fate as some would say. But mostly I believe it is the ability to think and react quickly, to remain calm under pressure and just get it done.

To conclude, it is a much different world today from the one I grew up in as a minor and young adult. But in many ways, it is more challenging and dangerous. At time of writing, the War Against Terror continues across the planet. However, the West seems to have triumphed over the evil menace of terrorism, lately ISIS has been gutted, their caliphate defeated and their top leader finally eliminated. Al Baghdadi was tracked to his hideout in Syria, in an area controlled by opposing Moslem groups. It is believed the U.S. Delta Force after being alerted to his location, stormed his compound, killed his guards, captured a few and a tracker dog led them to his underground hide. Cornered and knowing the game was up, the terrorist leader blew himself up. It remains to be seen if ISIS can replace their losses and be a factor in terrorist attacks in the future.

My advice is to those who seek it, regarding military service is test yourself, find your strengths and weaknesses, a passion for whatever it is that excites you, research it and master it. It could be as a serviceman, but also an athlete, skydiver, mountain climber, scuba diver, adventurer, pilot, academic or astronaut. As humans, it is our ongoing pursuit of the unknown, to push out new boundaries, pushing the envelope as soldiers and pilots call it, that lead to future success. For out there some thing or someone is and has been watching our progress.

Appendix A

Here I would like to discuss what many have experienced, close calls where one could perish or be severely injured. It is the one constant that has followed me throughout my life. I call it a phenomenon, highlighted recently in the series The UnXplained on History Channel. One night I watched the episode focussing on near death experiences. Several people spoke of an out of body experience and were clinically dead at the time. They recalled in vivid detail seeing their dead bodies, as their spirit hovered overhead. Some see their life flashing before their eyes, recalling loved ones or scenes from their past lives. I never experienced this myself, what I did feel was an invisible pull, as I felt death near, like a physical force pulling me into a dark abyss. Afterward it hit me, I was near death, escaping somehow that is unexplained.

This began early, I was around three years old and living in Toronto. I was racing my tricycle against some of my young mates, when I hit a curb and toppled into the street. I cracked my head on the pavement, cutting the top of my head. As I sat up, rubbing my aching skull, I saw a car coming at me. I froze in fear, thinking this was the end I suppose. I heard the screech of brakes, miraculously it missed me by inches. My buddies rushed out and pulled me to my feet and slapped my back as the driver checked me out. Later I sat on the porch, rubbing my head. My father came out and saw I was sitting quietly, asking me if everything was O.K. He saw the cut and drove me to the doctor. As I sat on the exam table, the doctor pulled at the cut, asking if it hurt. I did not say anything, but threw my first punch, popping him in the nose. My Dad related the story many times to a laughing crowd.

Shortly after this, Dad drove my older brother and myself to visit Great Uncle Charlie McCauley, who lived on a farm near Ottawa. Dad was probably learning the trade, as Charlie was running a pig farm then. We helped out with chores though we were very young. It was summer, Charlie was harvesting the crops, including hay and oats. One afternoon, Dad was helping Great Uncle Charlie load hay into the barn loft. It was 1960's and the hay was loose on the wagon. To transfer it to the loft, he rigged a huge fork, suspended by a cable to an overhead pulley, the free end attached to his old Ford tractor. Dad directed Charlie as he backed up, pulling the fork up after grabbing a load of hay. He was in his 70's then and hard of hearing, so when Dad told him to stop, he failed to hear it. I stood nearby a spectator to the scene, holding on to my bag of chips. I looked from the wagon, to the tractor puttering slowly out of the barn, then to the wire cable stretched taught, then up at the overhead forks.

"Oh oh!" I thought knowing something was not good, for the load was almost directly above my little head. I felt I was not in my happy place. The forks opened at the top, dumping the load of hay into the loft. This was good, going to plan I thought happily. But Charlie was still moving the tractor out of the barn stretching the cable tighter and tighter. I heard Dad shout ominously, "Sean! Get the heck out of there!" Again I froze, rooted to the floor, as panic set in. Seconds later, the cable snapped, my eyes staring blankly as the massive fork buried into the ground a foot away or so, missing me by inches. My biggest fear was Dad was displeased, fight or flight took over and my legs sped me to safety, dropping my bag of chips as I flew out of the barn, as if I had wings. I think my near miss being skewered like a pickle scared Charlie and Dad more than me. But I learned from it, never standing near those hideous forks again. Another time I was nearly devoured by Charlie's huge sows, after getting my rubber boots stuck in the pig yard. It was like visiting the Zoo for me, I wanted to pet the animals. I stood rooted in the muck, again holding a sack of chips, my favourite snack. The pigs as they closed in wanted me for a snack. For some reason, I did not cry, scream or shout for help. Then magically I escaped an ugly end, as Dad reached over the fence, gripped my shirt and yanked me out to safety. He set me down before him, smiling as he patted my head. I was staring at the pigs, my boots still lodged in the mud. "Thanks Daddy...could you get my boots please...and a bag of chips?"

We moved to the farm from Toronto in the 60's, where more near misses occurred. My brothers and I used to construct rafts every spring. We lived near the Nation River, a tributary of the Ottawa River. It would flood every year, submerging the fields around our house completely, converting it to an island, my mates called it Gilligan's Island after the show. Many times as we sailed the seas in our raft, we almost drowned. Near the river the current bucked and rocked the raft, sometimes sinking it. Luckily we had learned to swim, gasping as we made the shore wet and shivering. It never stopped us of course, we just learned to build more robust rafts that could withstand the punishment and stay afloat. It would stand me in good stead later. To this day fear of drowning and ocean predators is my biggest fear.

My Dad ran a dairy farm then, with a growing herd of cows and steers. Dad taught us to shoot as wolves, bears and moose were in the surrounding woods. I was out hunting one day with my brother, when I saw it. A big black bear in the brush, charging right at us. I had the 30-30 Winchester loaded, so let off a round. It missed of course, but the bear decided we were off the menu. It veered off, disappearing into the foliage as we stood rooted to the ground. Do you see what I see here? Is that pure blind luck or fate rearing it's head?

At any rate, these were the highlights of my life on the farm, except for the time I was nearly stomped to death by a nervous cow I was unhooking from the stall after milking. Again Dad was there to haul me to safety, bruised and covered in cow dung. Off I went to see Mom, who gasped at her filthy son. "Oh my, Sean...dear dear. OK strip off those clothes and take a bath this minute." I nodded, a bit chagrined and obeyed, more embarrassed than anything.

My first time driving was on that farm too. My uncle Connor had presented my older brother and myself with his old 1960's era Volkswagen as a present. Overjoyed we listened as he explained how to drive it, as it was a standard, brake, clutch, accelerator and stick shift. It took some learning, Mike being first to pick up the skill. I was a bit slower, but got it running down the road, hitting third gear as I rounded a turn in the rural dirt road. I whooped in triumph, then Mike told me to pull into an upcoming gate. I geared down and pulled in, but forgot about the brake. He yelled a warning...too late. The front hit the gate post and we came to a sudden stop. Thank the gods for excellent German engineering! Mike took over and it started up no problem, driving back to our farm, no harm no foul! Later we ripped off the dented up body with the tractor and converted it into a dune buggy.

As I grew older, I developed my shooting skills, mainly killing small game, pests like rats and ground hogs of course and to some regret the odd stray cat. We also killed the odd cow or pig for slaughter, giving us meat for the next year or so. I actually shot my first gun at the tender age of five. It was during my Austrian uncle's visit to hunt partridge on our farm. He unfortunately did not tell me to tuck the shotgun stock firmly into my shoulder. When it went off, it knocked me flat on my back. I lay there rubbing my sore shoulder as he made light of it.

These skills were going to be an asset later, when I joined the Canadian Armed Forces in my late teens. For a soldier who can not shoot accurately, is not much use in training or war. I learned to respect weapons, they were not toys, they had one purpose only, to kill something you aimed at. I had many fellow recruits who had no previous skill, some were dangerous and near misses were routine. Once on a range shoot, I was in a line of shooters, armed with the 9mm SMG. It was a short barrelled sub machine gun, designed for close quarter combat, with a 30 round magazine I believe. They are not used today and it was never my favourite weapon, no good for close quarter combat and short range. We were moving closer to the targets, maybe 50 meters away. As we waited the order to fire, our weapons on automatic, I looked over and saw the man beside me casually wiping his glasses with one hand, the other pointed the barrel directly at my face, his finger on the trigger.

"Sergeant MacDonald! A word please..." I ducked out of this fool's line of fire as the range NCO walked toward me, ordering weapons on safe. This man was not a Regular soldier, but a reservist (part-time), or 'weekend warriors' as the Regs called them. I told Mac what the fool was doing, unbelievably he was still waving that barrel around unaware he could have just blown my head off. Sergeant Mac was cool headed, taking the man off the range for further consultation, then we returned to our shooting without further incident. Later when I was Range NCO, I kicked a recruit off the range for repeatedly dropping his FN C1 in the dirt after firing a round. This rifle (no longer in service) had a decent kick and was fairly heavy at around twelve pounds with a 20- round magazine. It was my personal weapon for most of my service, as well as the automatic version, the FN C2, which had a bipod, used as a section's automatic in the fire base during assaults. It was also heavier, the soldier armed with six of the magazines, so in the field carried more weight and rounds. For this reason, newer guys (FNG's) had the unfortunate task of lugging it around, for a month at a time in the bonnies.

My next big 'near miss' was a vehicle roll over, around 1982 before I went to 3 Commando. I was with the Cameron Highlanders then, during a weekend exercise in CFB Petawawa, we were training with the armoured six wheeled Grizzly carrier. It carried a section of ten men and the driver, so was fairly big. Today the army uses a newer eight wheeled carrier, also replacing the old American built M-113 tracked carrier, which we used in Germany and other bases. The Grizzly had a turret, which could mount two machine guns, as commander of the vehicle I was in charge, sitting in the turret. I guy named Gagnon was the driver. We were travelling down a newly built road at night and it was raining. I was in communication with the driver using radio headsets. I was briefed by my boss, RSM Murphy who warned us not to get the heavy vehicle near the edge of the road. The Engineers had recently constructed this dirt road and the edges were not compacted yet. The Grizzly was a bit top heavy as well with the turret. As we topped a ridge, I looked down the road through the rain, the driver with his foot to the metal as they say. "Slow down Gagnon and stay in the center of the road."

As we proceeded down the embankment, he started to drift toward the right, near the edge, where I saw a deep ditch. The warning signs hit me immediately, thinking he did not hear me, I repeated the order, raising my voice to display the urgency. Alas, he did not head my warning, I felt the vehicle start to sink as the wheels dug into the soft sand. "Everybody get down! Brace for roll over." I ducked inside the open hatch, just as the Grizzly flipped over and rolled into the ditch. I have heard of incidents in Afghanistan where this had happened, killing the man in the turret, who did not duck down in time. As I lay in the bottom of the turret, the radio beside my head ripped off, smashing into the bulkhead beside me. Luckily, I was wearing my full rain suit for I was sprayed with battery acid. I looked around as the other guys were struggling in the back, smoke and dust everywhere.

"Private open the rear door! Everyone out now! Move move!" Luckily all ten men safely evacuated the vehicle, rain drenching us as I looked at the six wheels pointing up at the night sky. I told the RSM about it later, advising me to charge the driver with negligence. He also had his army driver's license taken away and banned from driving. Strangely enough, my next near miss happened not far away and was also a vehicle roll over. It was my first real car, a 1975 Dodge Coronet and I was driving it down a gravel road toward base in Petawawa's outback. It was 1984, now I was a paratrooper in 3 Commando. It was a beautiful car and I was showing it off to Gary Vienneau, one of my 10 Platoon buddies. We had just been to a beach party on the Ottawa River, to send off one of our guys who was releasing from the forces.

Admittedly I was going too fast for the conditions, going over a rise I felt the wheels leave the road. The next thing I remember was lying in hospital, with a doctor stitching up a gash on my left temple. Gary told me later, we had rolled three times into the ditch. I cut my head apparently on the side door. I was young but had used my seatbelt, ultimately that saved my life. If I had not, I would have been thrown out the window and crushed to death. I recall this one vividly, as I still have the scar there today. It is a good talking piece at social events, like my other scars, I am proud to have them. The doctors all did a good job stitching me up, none of your nasty, crudely stitched affairs. Nice and smooth and not marring my good looks much.

After the Doc stitched me up, I returned to duty immediately, as I was not badly injured. I was lucky again, unlike my car. I found it at an Auto shop in the village, where the mechanic told me it was a right off. I actually got it running and was reluctant to let it go. After talking to my older brother Mike, we went car shopping the next week. I purchased my second car in Ottawa, at Mike's advice, a 1980 Ford Mustang with a 4-cylinder engine. I upgraded after a year changing to a 6-cylinder engine, bigger brakes, wheels and twin exhausts for better power.

During this time, I was heavily involved in aquatic sports, being an accomplished swimmer since my early days on the farm. Based in Petawawa, we were a stone's throw from several rivers. We had many occasions to hit the beach on the Ottawa River. During one celebration to celebrate the anniversary of the liberation of Rome, we drank wine to toast it. It popped into my head, as I watched the sun set, to swim across the river to the Quebec side.

Off I went, easily getting half way across, then trouble reared its head. I felt an undertow, the current catching me and trying to pull me under. I was on my own, as my buddies decided wisely not to join me. I aborted the journey to the far side, turning around and digging for the party side. The current which was shielded up till now by a turn in the river and the headland to the south, now had me in it's grasp. It swept me downstream to the north, as the undertow like a hand tried to pull me under and drown me. I was pushed to my limits, eventually getting out of the current, struggling to the west bank some time later. I was gutted as I made the beach, gasping for air, thanking the gods for mercy. It was some time later before I made it to the party, a drunken girl hugged me, asking where I had been. "Why do you look stressed out Sean? Ah you want hug?" I smiled hugging her, quickly forgetting my near miss.

I followed this up, during another weekend trip, this time with my mates, checking out the waterfalls on the Petawawa River. Many have drowned here, but danger was our middle name. Someone had come up with the great idea of going over the falls using our field air mattresses. After watching the first guy hurtle over and live, I finished my early morning beer. I inflated my air mattress and launched it upstream from the falls. We had planned to drift down to a big rock, then hit the falls dead on. I reached the rock and grabbed for it to steady and turn the head to the falls. It was covered in slippery moss, then the current caught my air mattress. My hands slipped off the rock, gasping as I headed toward the roaring falls...sideways!

    I gasped as I hung on for dear life, hurtled over the falls and vanished into the maelstrom, thinking maybe this was not a good idea for a Saturday morning after all. I plunged below the surface, the air mattress was ripped from my hands, maybe by Poseidon, Greek god of the seas? I recall being sucked into a whirlpool at the bottom of the falls. My immediate thought as I twirled around in that maelstrom of roaring water was, "I am dead! Not getting out of this one buddy!" I do not know what happened in the following seconds, but I did not struggle, the power of water as I knew was immense. To struggle against it was hopeless, so resigned to my fate, I awaited Poseidon finishing off this hapless mortal. Then unexpectedly, I was spat out of the whirlpool. I bounced off rocks downstream, finally my head broke the surface, gasping for air. I caught hold of a rock, but the current again whipped me away. I was barefoot as well, also a mistake, as I could get no solid purchase against the rocks, cutting my feet in the process. Some of my buddies shouted from the bank, following my progress down the Petawawa 'death slide" River. Eventually having survived the gauntlet I reached a slower moving body of water and extricated myself. My buddies escorted me back to our camp, handing me beer and slapping my back. I was gutted as I lay on my back swilling beer, as some girls attended to my wounds. "Never again Mate! Higgins you and your crazy ideas!"

My next thing was a hard landing, during a mass drop from Hercules aircraft onto DZ Anzio. Having recently attained jump status with my 'white wings,' it was a routine administrative jump. It was a bit windy though, coming down under the round parachute, I was blown backwards. It was my first like this, though we had trained for it in jump school. I looked over my shoulder, seeing I was headed for an old shell crater, as this was an artillery range before W.W. 1, 75 years before that day. I did not panic though, tucked my chin in to my chest and braced for landing. I hit the top of the crater, rolling backwards, cartwheeling 'arse over tea kettle', like a human ball rolling down the crater slope. I had equipment attached to my harness, so it was a rough landing. I got up O.K. but felt a bit woozy as I climbed out of the hole.

In the end, I was medivacked to hospital, thankfully as I missed the rucksack march back to base over 10 miles away. After a quick ride to the base, medics took X-rays, informing me nothing was broke, but I had a compressed disc in my neck. This was something new, as I did not know how my spine worked, hence I learned from it. In effect, as I understand it, there are discs between each segment of the spinal cord, acting as cushions. Hence, they move and compress, cushion the bone from hitting each other and or pinching the vital spinal cord. If this is fractured, the result is permanent damage, usually paralysis. I had a buddy, Sly Sylvester, who I mentioned earlier, suffer temporary paralysis.

This was during the winter of 1984, the morning after I jumped onto Round Lake, Ontario for my first fully tactical night, full equipment jump with the Airborne, having passed my Basic Para the previous December. I saw Sly shortly after he landed, seeing he was in some pain, he was walking around but clearly not 100 per cent. "Damn it. I landed on my machine gun Sean. My freaking back is sore." Shortly after he collapsed and was medivacked out to hospital. When we returned to base after the exercise ended weeks later, the boys from our Commando visited him in hospital. He explained he had paralysis in his back and unable to move his legs. It was scary, as the doctors did not know if it was permanent or not. Thankfully he was lucky, about a month later the paralysis faded and he was walking around on crutches. Soon after he was released, began rehab and rejoined 3 Commando later that spring.

We were tight Sly and I, when he said he was scared to jump again, I backed him up. Saying things like, "take your time dude, but you must get back in the game." Some time later he jumped with us, everything was good. But this was an eye opener, parachuting was a serious thing, potentially dangerous even with a good chute. I know of guys who were not as lucky in my time in the Borne. One Major I believe, from E Battery thundered in, after another chute "stole his air" during a mass drop on DZ Anzio. We heard him scream as his main chute collapsed a few hundred feet above the deck. He hit hard, breaking allot of bones, including his back and both femurs but lived, although I heard later he was done as a paratrooper. I never heard anything more of him, his jumping days done forever. I know to those who have never jumped, this will probably not convince you to try it. My response is, civilian skydiving is not nearly as demanding, though there is still inherent risks involved, as any sport has, especially extreme sports. People have died playing rugby, football and hockey. The worst case was the junior hockey team from Humboldt Saskatchewan, when a speeding transport went through a stop sign and rammed into their bus. A dozen killed and most of the team injured, some permanently. I ask you, is there a perfectly safe sport or hobby?

    I heard of some poor old guy who died playing golf, after he rolled his golf cart into a water obstacle. It flipped over, pinning him under water and he drowned. But back to my near misses, the next notable one occurring in 1985. It was right after boot camp in Dundurn, Saskatchewan. The Airborne jumped into RV 85 in Wainwright, Alberta early one morning. 3 Commando's DZ was at Rifle Ridge. It was pitch black and raining as I came down under my chute. As it was fully tactical, we were briefed to carry the maximum of weapons, ammunition, water and rations, as we would not be resupplied for at least a week. I could not see the ground, as I released my gear, I could just make out a few shadowy forms nearby, other paratroopers. We shouted to each other, the usual routine keeping us alert.

I hit the ground after a few seconds and rolled. As I lay there I sensed something was amiss, even though I did not feel any pain. A low level throbbing in my leg, I thought, ah no big deal, probably tweaked a ligament. The chute came down right on top of me as I struggled to extract the rigging lines that entangled me. Then feeling my leg, I felt a twinge of fear. My left thigh was wet and even worse something was sticking out of it. I felt the object, as I could see nothing, tracing along it to my leg. "Oh oh...shit!" It hit me, my rifle the FN which had a long barrel had penetrated through my leg and was lodged there. Also, I had an open wound where it exited and I was bleeding. I was also buried under my chute and could not move. Eventually I pulled the chute off enough to yell for assistance. I squeezed the wound trying to staunch the blood loss. I stayed calm though, not resorting to screaming and crying for my mother.

Eventually Trooper Crawford arrived, I explained briefly what I knew and required medical assistance ASAP. Soon after Medic Randy Corchoran arrived and began to treat my injury. He calmed me as he talked, saying lay back and relax. With the assistance of other paratroopers, my gear and chute harness was stripped off and carried away. Randy slid the FN out of my leg, then quickly and expertly bandaged it up. He said he thought no bones were fractured and it missed the femoral artery. If this had even been nicked, I would have died after a minute or so, bleeding out rapidly. A group of 3 Commando soldiers gathered around me as Randy fixed an inflatable brace to immobilize my leg. It was decided to medivac me out on an ambulance, not a helicopter. I joked I was clearly not important enough to get out on a chopper. I was still not in allot of pain, blissfully ignorant of the severity of my injury.

"Heck Warrant just strap on a peg and I will rejoin my platoon and walk out of this shit." He smiled and said that was not going to happen, patted my shoulder and walked off. Four guys lifted up my stretcher and off we went across the remote Rifle Ridge to the evac zone. I was resigned to the ambulance which arrived some time later. We where in the outback of the base, no roads hence it was a bumpy ride. As I bounced up and down the pain started and got progressively worse as I had not been given any pain killer drugs yet. I cursed the driver who threatened to dump me out, so I grinned and beared it. After gritting my teeth, a medic consoled me, handing me a cigarette to calm my nerves. At the hospital, I then had to wait hours, for they had no doctor competent enough for anything other than basic surgery I suppose. Stripped of my gear and clothing, I lay on a slab for hours as medics poked and prodded at me. A nurse cleaned the worst of the grime I was coated in, then I saw my thigh wound! It freaked me out, for it was split open from above the knee for a foot and a half or so.

It was also crammed with mud so was not bleeding a lot. I joked with the nurse to take my mind off of it, saying she was getting a free chance to grope me, as I was totally naked. "I have seen it all before soldier," the usual response I joked. I saw the old D-Day movie with John Wayne later. One scene shows a downed Spitfire Pilot, played by Richard Harris, had a similar wound. A paratrooper from the U.S. Screaming Eagles (101st Division), separated from his unit, stumbled on the injured pilot, giving him a cigarette. "The medic who patched me up lost his first aid kit. So he closed my wound with safety pins. No pain killers of course."[8]

The civilian doctor finally arrived early that morning. He was awesome, settling me down, assuring me he could handle this. We joked around a bit before they put me under. My last parting words being, "I just want to see that leg there in the morning Doc." He laughed and nodded, adding cleaning the wound thoroughly was most important, to prevent infection. He would then examine it, before stitching me up, hopefully nothing was broken.

It all turned out as planned, I awoke hours later in a field hospital intensive care ward. The Doctor came in, saying all went well, the next thing being to monitor the leg and change bandages regularly. I nodded, mentioning this was not my first wound. Shell fragments had sliced open my kneecap in West Germany six years earlier.

---

8   from the movie 'The Longest Day'

The similarity was I could have got infection, leading to gangrene and amputation. Theoretically you can die from this, if not treated correctly. Alas with modern medical knowledge and antibiotics (like penicillin), this is getting more rare. Unlike during WW 1 and before, getting infection was almost always fatal.[9]

I was confined to bed for a few weeks, until the medics declared I was good to go and start rehabbing, first on crutches. It was hard at first, as my muscles had atrophied as I lay in bed with minimal movement. However I displayed my ability to recover quickly, soon returning to the skies about two months later. In the end I completely recovered, adding another scar to my collection. I also had my buddies in the platoon to rely on, my family and girl friend in Ottawa to ease me back into the world. Around this time, to ease the worry of my loved ones, I declared, "Ah don't worry I can't die. I am a demi-god. I can only die from another god's hand." Of course, there was Alexander the Great and Achilles, both believed to be gods, who died fairly young under mysterious circumstances. Probably from an infected

---

[9] During the American Civil War, General Stonewall Jackson, one of the Confederate's leading Generals was shot by mistake by one of his own men after winning a battle, a casualty of friendly fire. He was hit in the arm, medivacked and survived. But infection set in, his arm was subsequently amputated. He died after days in agony, also catching pneumonia, finishing off the stalwart, fearless warrior.

wound as both had been in battle many times prior to dying. One account says King Alexander was shot by an archer during a siege, which could have caused a slow, lethal wound. Today thankfully arrows are not used, replaced by other more destructive weapons, including mass destruction.

My next near miss occurred in Cyprus that fall. It happened during a night patrol, on the Ormophita Plains, in no man's land between the two opposing Greek/Turk forces. I was there with 3 Commando, who had joined 2 RCHA, as the Canadian peacekeeping contingent. As U.N. peacekeepers, we were lightly armed, carrying one magazine with 20 rounds for our rifles. We were not allowed to load the rifle without an officer's direct order, whether we were engaged or not. Essentially we were non-combatants, free game for the trigger happy, poorly trained Cypriot militia we encountered frequently. It happened suddenly, a shot cracked out and I heard the whizz close to my helmet. My blue UN marked 'tin pot' helmet could have stopped a BB gun pellet, but not much else. I thought I was dead for a moment, then I hit the ground next to the radioman, realizing I was alive. He called in to the Ops call sign, requesting support.

I tried locating the shooter, but it was pitch black out and saw nothing. As I was sniper trained, I looked for good firing positions, while crawling for cover. There where destroyed buildings all around us, as this had been an active war zone. There were also booby traps everywhere, unexploded ordnance and mine fields. I knew at that moment, this was it. I was in combat at last! As I awaited orders to kill the bastard who had tried to kill me, I loaded my FN. I grinned at the radioman, hissing at him, trying to contain my fear, adrenaline and excitement. Luckily I guess, the shooter did not fire another round, or I would have returned fire, orders or no. An officer arrived shortly after, consulted with the Greek Cypriots manning their nearby positions. I was informed after returning to base for debriefing, that the offender was a nervous Greek Cypriot militia sentry. He claimed he thought he was firing at a stray dog.

An obvious lie, or he was really dumb, as he was firing in the direction of the Turkish lines some distance to the east. If they had returned fire, he would have caused a major incident, if not all out battle. I would have been in the free fire zone in the middle, so it was another near miss. Later I was diagnosed with a sort of PTSD, as I had anger issues, lack of patience with fools and a short-term memory loss. Some names I forget almost immediately. Except if she is hot! For me, the worst part was frustration with U.N. rules of engagement. We were expendable guinea pigs, having to be fired at while we waited permission to defend our selves. I survived this tour and received my medal back home in Canada months later.

That was my last real near miss with death in the army, but not my last injury. It was also in Cyprus during my skydives with the Brit freefall team, when I had another near miss. I was descending under my main chute to the DZ's target landing area. A freak gust of wind blew me off the target and I headed toward the nearby DZ shack, with a big, pointy wind vane and aerial sticking up at me as I approached. I tucked my knees up, as this was an obstacle. I landed fortuitously directly on the roof, ran across it, missed the pointy objects and landed on the far side, amazingly on my feet. I looked down to where a Brit jumper looked up at me, wide eyed as he packed his chute. "Sorry mate" I, replied nonchalantly and strolled off grinning.

Also during this time, our platoon was in the athletic center, to take the Ranger swim test. We went off the diving board, wearing full combat gear. Of course, we plunged to the bottom, then similar to the Navy Seal's swim test, one held their breath as they stripped off their gear and ascended to the surface. Then if all was O.K., swam a lap around the pool.

I had no problem here, having survived harsher tests in the Petawawa and Ottawa Rivers. One of my section mates though, had a problem. He was pulled out of the pool unconscious as some performed CPR. We were relieved when he finally regained consciousness after a minute or so. He remarked coolly, "I was in no danger guys. I knew you lads would pull me though!" It was a sign of Airborne brotherhood at work. My last injury was when I fractured my ankle during RV 87 in Wainwright.

As it was not life threatening I will not go into any further detail. After my release in 1987 in London, Ontario I was back with the masses of civilian life once more. I went quite a long time before my next near miss, but was injured the following year playing rugby with The City of London's team.

It was my first season playing full time in a civilian rugby league team. I had limited experience beginning in Cyprus in 1985, playing a fun game. 3 Commando vs. the Welsh Guards, both based in Cyprus for a six-month tour. I was a football player at a university level, so rugby was a new sport. 3 Commando played Canadian city teams over the rest of my tour (1985-86), but I was still a novice playing for London. I was put in as a prop, front row in the scrum. Props are like football linemen, meaning they should be the biggest guys, well over six feet and two hundred pounds. I am not, around 5'11," at this time around 180 pounds.

One game, it got to me, my sternum, the cartilage holding the ribcage together, was torn open. As the scrum came apart, I fell into the mud gasping for breath as the rest of the team went tearing across the field. It was like I was knifed in the chest, I thought I might be dying. Eventually I crawled off the field (without any medical assistance), went to the hospital, where a doctor diagnosed it a cartilage injury, saying he could do nothing. It would take a year or so to repair itself, in the mean time take it easy, no rugby or contact sports.

I finished my studies at college in London, moving to Toronto metro area in 1990, working there after graduation.

Fast forward to 2000, I had graduated from Carleton University in Ottawa, then moved out west to Winnipeg. That summer while working at CFB Shilo, I re-entered the parachuting world after a decade long hiatus. After doing the Basic first jump, I kept going, aiming to get my Solo license. It took a while, as it was not my main focus. Then on October 8, my seventh jump that year, 26th skydive overall, I had a near miss. It was just a normal jump from 4000 feet with a 5 second delay. I was still not licensed, so still technically a novice (beginner) jumper. I exited by myself, delayed five seconds as I fell. I was not yet at terminal speed, this takes longer (up to 15 seconds), then I reached for ripcord to pull and deploy the pilot chute but it did not come out. I tried again, in fact several times, which is a beginner's mistake. I was lucky again though, as I reached lower altitude the AAD fired the reserve. It opened at or below a thousand feet, as I looked momentarily at the ground, I could see the ground rushing up. Momentarily in a split second, I thought I am in a bad place, I could be dead in seconds. As I reached for the reserve handle I heard a pop, looked up and saw the reserve chute come out, billowing open at over 500 feet. I yanked on the toggle lines, flared and amazingly had a soft landing, standing up in a field at the far end of Gimli's DZ.

An instructor landed soon after, asking me if I was OK. I nodded, walking back to the DZ building, thinking over what had just happend. It ended up as my last jump that year. My next jump was on Canada Day in 2001 at Steinbach, the other DZ in Manitoba. I worked on practicing short delays, learning from past mistakes and building confidence. I ended up at 30 jumps that year and felt I was back on track. In 2002 I moved to Edmonton which I call home today.

I began working in Alberta's oil and gas industry, which is demanding, taking me all over the vast Prairies. It was mostly surveying work with some facility maintenance, then Service rigs, maintaining well sites. I began jumping once more at Eden North DZ west of Edmonton. It went well, finally awarded my first Solo license I did my first full freefall from 11,500 feet in June, fifteen more that summer, qualifying for a Solo license in August. I had 50 skydives since I began in the 1980's but I now had confidence I could do this. Today new skydivers can do it much faster, with better chutes, instructors and bigger, faster planes. It is not cheap though, running into the thousands, with purchasing your own equipment easily running into four figures. So, it is not for everyone, only the committed.

Then I switched DZ's again, to Westlock, north of Edmonton. I was doing survey work in the area, felt the need to check it out, so that weekend in late August did my first jump there. I ended up calling it my home

DZ for the next fifteen years, though I jumped at many other DZ's, including B.C. I attained my A license that fall, enabling me to jump in more complex, bigger groups and compete in competitions. I continued improving but still was not there yet. I had several reserve openings, including so called 'two -out" around 2005. This was not good, as the two chutes could have tangled and led to a roman candle, from which there is not much one can do to extricate yourself. So technically this was a close call, but I landed on the DZ without a scratch, casually laughing off the dire warnings I heard from other jumpers.

In 2007 I purchased my first jump rig, with a PD 230 main chute, completing my B rating in October at Westlock. I had over 200 skydives now and it was becoming indelibly etched in my life and persona. My main finally blew up the following year, splitting along a cell after a hard opening. By now this was not a huge deal. I cutaway promptly and pulled my reserve. I landed on the DZ again without a scratch. Riggers advised me not to repair it, as it was from the 1980's, therefore likely to fail again. I borrowed chutes for a while, then replaced my main with a Sabre 1 main. It was a match made in heaven, since then I have no malfunctions or reserve rides on my rig to this day. The problem was I have tried other chutes to see if I wanted to downsize further. My last reserve was about six years ago, when I experimented with a 170, a bit smaller and faster than mine. I jumped with it a few times, but the last time that day, as it was getting dark, it tried to kill me. It opened OK, then started twisting the lines, then it dived toward the ground. I did not panic however, as I was still over 2000 feet. I cut it away, then pulled the reserve handle. I executed a pin-point landing on the target and stood up fine. The chute disappeared into the night unfortunately. Luckily, I found it the next day in a nearby field, or would have had to buy the owner a new chute (starting at $6-7000). It cost me about $80 for the rigger to repack his reserve, in the end I decided to stick with my Sabre main chute.

Finally in 2017, I had my final close call. It was in early September at Westlock on Labour Day. That week my main chute was in for repair, requiring new suspension lines, after one broke. I borrowed another 170 main as I was competing in an Accuracy jump meet that weekend. It went well and I felt confident and at the top of my game. I could handle just about anything I thought happily. The next day on a holiday Monday I returned to the DZ for some fun jumping. On my first jump that afternoon, jump number 465, it happened. I was also pushing for 500 jumps that year, an important milestone in one's career.

The jump went perfect, up until I was below 100 feet above the DZ, preparing to land. I was aiming for the accuracy target, which I had done the previous day several times. The next thing I knew, I was lying prone on my back on the ground. I had apparently hit hard, knocking me out, therefore I had a nasty concussion to start with. A medic and a few people stood over me looking concerned. My first words were, "What are you guys doing? Practicing?"

Nobody laughed and I was told not to move, as they were checking me for injuries. I remarked I was feeling no pain anywhere, unknown to me then I had just had my worst accident ever. I argued when they tried cutting off my jumpsuit, my one and only camouflage one of a kind suit, I had bought years before. I was eventually strapped to a stretcher and medivacked out in an Alberta Emergency ambulance. Eventually I arrived at a hospital in Edmonton for further evaluation, after the Westlock hospital said they could not do the surgery. It was my first trip to the ER in Edmonton since moving there.

Queen Alexandra Hospital took me into the Emergency Room, where I was x-rayed. Doctors told me later my left tibia was shattered, my knee needed reconstruction and both wrists were badly fractured. I could not believe it at first. I lay in bed confused and stunned the next morning as nurses flitted about and doctors visited. I had two major operations over the next three weeks, but in the end, it turned out as well as can be expected. By the fourth week, I knew I would make it, with all limbs attached. But would I be able to jump again?

As I recuperated slowly, some of my jump buddies visited me, raising my flagging morale, insisting I was not done yet. Travis my good friend even snuck me in a pack of cigarettes and some beer. Travis, his girlfriend Ana and I spent some time during their weekly visits at the outside smoking patio. While relaxing there, I saw other patients, some not as lucky as me. There were amputees and others in clearly poor physical states. I shook my head as Travis smiled,

"See those guys dude? Thankfully I am not a mortal!" We laughed at my joke. I was on crutches by the seventh week, recovering nicely, but was eager to get back to the world. I lived in a townhouse alone, was paying the bills on my cell phone and credit card, but was nervous about my house unattended. Finally, after seven weeks in hospital, I was released after urging the doctor to let me go. I still had casts on my arms as my wrists had not healed fully. I could stand on my legs though and passed a final test on my crutches. A neighbour picked me up in mid-October and finally I returned home. The rest of 2017 was a battle, but I persevered, even on my own. In February 2018, I finally had the casts removed, but were still tender and weakened. I began a rehab program at the suggestion of my doctor. She was awesome, even suggesting it was up to me to get back into skydiving. I still was not confident I could, but the door was not slammed shut. My biggest worry was that now I had metal plates and screws in my leg and wrists permanently. If I reinjured them, the resulting operation and recovery would not be as fast.

That spring and into the summer I steadily improved, rehabbing in the gym several times a week. In June, I returned to Westlock DZ for the first time, talked to people about returning to skydiving and such. I listened to some sage advice, as they said take your time. Meanwhile I had bought a Winchester .30-06 rifle and joined the rifle club on Edmonton's army base. This was Option B if I was unable to return to the skydiving. It went well, my basic shooting skills were still intact and it was a relaxing, pleasurable hobby. I had also passed my firearms course and was licensed, early in 2017, before this last accident. It was part of life's journey, replacing old skills and sport with new ones.

Finally, in August of that summer, I made the call, jumping for the first time in almost a year. It went well, for by now the riggers had repaired my main and rig. Lesson number one here, be careful when borrowing a chute that is not your own. I slowly returned to full activity, using the base gym for full workouts, including swimming. Over the next two years no further accidents or problems, but switched DZ's again after Westlock closed. The new DZ is presently at Innisfail, 200 kilometers south of Edmonton. I had one hard landing, on the tarmac of the taxi lane. I fell and nicked up my leg and hands, but amazingly nothing serious. It was a test I had avoided like the plague, but I passed it. Unfortunately, I barely missed my long-time goal of 500 jumps, finishing just shy at 497, mainly due to unseasonably bad weather. The final weekend in October was a complete stop drop, with high winds, low ceiling and even snow. So, we did as jumpers everywhere do, we partied the night away to the wee hours of the next day. Next year, the gods being willing, I will easily surpass 500 and life will go on...C'est la vie.

In the meantime, I continue my passion for writing. Travel is also one of my lifelong pursuits. I flew to San Diego, California for the first time in March. Edmonton was in the last dregs of winter, cold and icy, a cold, desolate wasteland to me. California was much better, warmer and had beaches, being a Pacific state and further south. I had arranged for hotel and a rental car, arriving late Saturday evening at The Ramada Inn in National City. I had tried driving there in the spring of 2017 but bad weather had stopped me in Seattle.

The next day in California, I drove to the nearest drop zone at Otay Lakes near the Mexican border. I had to get a USPA license to jump there, but finally did my first California skydive late that day. Then bad weather closed in for the next day or so. I drove north that Wednesday to the DZ at Oceanside, between San Diego and Los Angeles to the north.

I borrowed jump rigs for this as I did not want to chance my own priceless rig to the airport security. I completed three skydives there, jumping over the city and getting a great view of the nearby beaches and the Pacific Ocean. I flew back home the following weekend, but it was a successful trip. Most importantly the landings were pain and injury free. I had insurance coverage just in case, but even a simple injury would have complicated my vacation. It was also a time to get to know this city, as it figured into my second book The Penal Regiment. I liked everything about that fabled port town, being a U.S. Naval Base, where I saw my first real aircraft carrier, The U.S.S. Midway. One can visit on board for a small fee, certainly recommended. This was also the home to Fighter town U.S.A. and Top Gun School.

Also, Camp Pendleton the U.S. Marine base, which I strayed onto as I was looking for a beach. The Marine guards turned me around, no harm no foul, as explained I was just another dumb Canuck visitor, but also a Canadian ex-soldier and Veteran. So, as I soaked in the rays, checked the local scene out and took notes for my book it was a pleasurable week.

For those who do not have any close calls, or near visits by the Grim Reaper, I can only say be patient, for he shall visit, sooner or later. Life is all about continual learning, embracing the dangers imposed by Earth and now space. I do not indulge in the morass of politics and social conflict. Instead I am immersed in a variety of sports and activities. Through my experiences, I have a healthy respect for death, cheating it if you will, many, many times. Hopefully this will eventually disappear, and I will die of old age and ease my transition into the afterlife, which visits us all eventually. In my case, my hope is a quick trip to Valhalla, Viking heaven for the bravest, fearless warriors. Demi-gods and Valhalla are a product of earlier man's imagination of course, to deal with the finality of death that faces all humans.

In this tale, I pass on my three decades long journey from a young, Canadian paratrooper, to an older civilian skydiver. I do believe that today, jumping is an important skill to have. Just as an example, Bear Grylls show on National Geographic called 'Running Wild.' In the latest show I watched as he made his guest star, Channing Tatum parachute into the northern wilderness of Norway. Bear states his aim is to instruct Tatum on modern survival skills in the wilderness. I salute Bear Grylls in his helping this actor gain valuable skills, I believe he learned as a Special Forces paratrooper in U.K.'s Army. I can humbly say, I learned something from his shows, but am repulsed by some of the things he forces his shocked guests to eat, including bugs, worms, dead road kill and eyeballs. I did eat rattle snake though during the Texas desert op and liked it, while Tatum says he didn't.

Appendix B: History of Parachuting

Parachuting originated during the First World War, as a means of saving early pilot lives. Up till then, if a plane caught fire or had engine problems, or other emergencies, everyone aboard was doomed, as the odds of surviving a crash were minimal. Military uses of the parachute were experimented with during the 1930's, leading to the first Airborne Parachute units, namely in Russia, Germany and England. The first use of the Airborne assault, occurred in May 1940 during the German Blitzkrieg in the second year of WW 2, when several gliders landed on the Belgian fort of Eben Emael, which was thought to be impregnable and seized it in hours. The German paratroopers were trained for months before executing this risky, surprise attack. They used new tactics and weapons, the assault glider and hollow charges to disable the guns of the elaborate Belgian fort. Simultaneously the German Army (Wehrmacht), used paratroopers to seize Dutch airfields and key bridges, leading to the rapid conquest of Western Europe in just over a month. The Allied nations were initially slow to acquire this new technology, but Britain established it's first paratrooper and Commando units in 1941, followed by U.S., Canada and Australia in 1942. The British Commandos launched several successful raids on German occupied Europe mainly in Norway and France. The word Commando was adopted from the Dutch Boers during the Boer War, for their small bands of raiders who fought the British in a guerilla style, non-traditional manner.

The 1st Canadian Parachute Battalion were the pioneers in Canada, the first paratroopers, established in 1942. They got their blooding two years later, during D-Day on June 6th, 1944, joining American and British Airborne divisions in establishing the first foothold in occupied France. After this successful intro, the Canadian paratroopers fought through France, then jumped across the Rhine River in 24th March of 1945, Operation Varsity. Five weeks later, the war ended and this first Canadian airborne unit was disbanded shortly after.

Acknowledgements

This book is firstly dedicated to my direct family, including my Mom, sister, nieces, nephews and three brothers (all who have parachuted safely). Also in memorium, for my Dad who passed away over a decade ago.

Secondly this is for my brothers, past and serving paratroopers in Canada, our Allies (U.S., U.K., NATO, Australia, New Zealand). But also, it is a read for any jump qualified soldier anywhere in the world. In Canada JTF-2 is the newest successor to the disbanded Airborne Regiment, 1st Canadian Parachute Battalion and The Devil's Brigade of WW 2. Also, each of Canada's three regular infantry battalions have a dedicated jump company. JSOR {Joint Special Operations Regiment} is the other parachute qualified army unit, recently joining JTF-2 in the Middle East "war on terror."

Lastly I should mention the members of Canada's CSPA, Canadian Sport Parachuting Association, some

3000-members in Canada. After I retired from the Canadian Forces in the 1980's, civilian skydiving replaced military jumps, keeping me going strong decades later. For those who have not jumped yet, this can inspire you or scare you away, I leave to the reader to decide if it is, or not for them.

Also for all those military jumpers who have sacrificed all for our protection and way of life. My final words to live by "train hard to stay in the game of life."

The Airborne Creed: What manner of men are these who wear the marron beret?

They are, firstly, all volunteers and are toughened by hard physical training. As a result they have that infectious optimism and that offensive eagerness which comes from physical well being. They have 'jumped' from the air and by doing so have conquered fear.

Their duty lies in the van of battle; they are proud of this honour and have never failed in any task. They have the highest standards in all things whether it be skill in battle in smartness in execution of all peace-time duties. They have shown themselves to be as tenacious and determined in defence as they are courageous in the attack. They are, in fact, men apart-every man an Emperor. Of all the factors which make for success in battle the spirit of the warrior is the most decisive. That spirit will be found in full measure in the men who wear the maroon beret.

Field Marshall
The Viscount Montgomery of Alamein

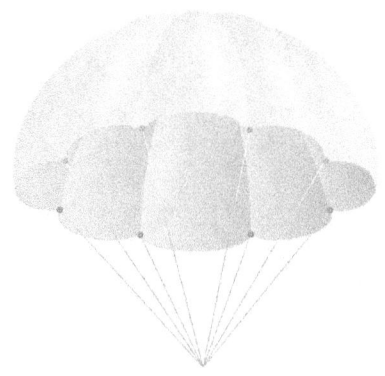

Bibliography/References

1. Into Icy Waters: by Tom MacGregor; Pg. 48-52; LEGION MAGAZINE MAY/JUNE 2018 LEGIONMAGAZINE.COM; Publisher: Canvet Publications Ltd.

2. HISTORY MAGAZINE: The Covert Missions of the Military's Elite Fighting Force November 2018

3. THE MAROON BERET Magazine, November 1985; Pg.1-48, Editor: Captain G.E. Thompson CD

4. 1st Canadian Parachute Battalion 50th Anniversary Magazine; June 1992; Pg. 115

5. Photos supplied by author, Tellwell Publications, Victoria B.C.

Photos

Author: Sean Gilligan on home leave from CFB Petawawa with Ford Mustang C. 1984
2000: Return to skydiving at Gimli, MB. 1st skydive in a decade. Thumbs up!

Sean Gilligan (author): *In Texas/ New Mexico desert with 3 Commando, Airborne Regiment, March 1985. First time training in desert operations. In Ex. Border Star later the full Airborne Battle Group executed a mass drop at night, acting as Enemy force for the U.S. 10th Mountain Division. At end-ex we celebrated a victorious conclusion.*

Exercise Border Star Texas Desert 1985: 10 Platoon, 3 Commando, Canadian Airborne Regiment: A case of a Few Good Men: 700 Paratroopers took on a US Light Mechanized Division of 15000 + US soldiers, tanks, choppers, armour tracked vehicles

Mass drop: Paratroopers performing a standard, fast exit from a C-17 Starlifter transport plane. This is the largest jump plane today, used by U.S.A.F. and Canadian Air Force. It can carry approx. 200 paratroopers plus equipment and light vehicles on pallets. Also alternately it can transport M-1 Abrams heavy tanks to any spot on Earth. I jumped from this and the Hercules transports during my Airborne tour. Ref. Pixabay website

www.ingramcontent.com/pod-product-compliance
Lightning Source LLC
LaVergne TN
LVHW011810060526
838200LV00053B/3721